100

THINGS TO DO IN

MISSOURI
BEFORE YOU
DIE

Katy Trail

100

THINGS TO DO IN

MISSOURI

BEFORE YOU

DIE

● ●

JOHN W. BROWN AND

AMANDA E. DOYLE

REEDY PRESS

Library of Congress Control Number: 2020922403

ISBN: 9781681062983

Design by Jill Halpin

Cover image: Courtesy of Dogwood Canyon
Photos by authors or in the public domain unless otherwise noted.

Printed in the United States of America
21 22 23 24 25   5 4 3 2 1

DEDICATION

JWB: To my wife and girls, thanks for visiting so many
of these places with me. We have a lot more to see. And to all my
Show-Me State friends, the pandemic made us realize we should
never take a nice Missouri weekend for granted again!

AED: To my lifelong friends from Mizzou—I keep you all
in my heart, even those who went far afield. You always
have a spot at my Missouri table!

Boulevard Brewing

CONTENTS

• •

Music and Entertainment

Sports and Recreation

• •

Culture and History

• •

• •

Shopping and Fashion

Great Main Streets and Neighborhoods

Marvel Cave

PREFACE

There are plenty of ways you can get to know a place.

John grew up all across Missouri, while Amanda arrived as a transplant, and we both agree that the Show-Me State is packed with a dizzying array of gems—from small-town main streets to big-city cultural happenings—that should be shouted from the top of Taum Sauk Mountain! The two of us have, combined, written or broadcast dozens of books, articles, and stories about a place we both love: Missouri.

Working on recent projects, we found ourselves longing to revisit places we'd been away from.

As John says: "While I was writing *Missouri: An Illustrated Timeline*, I found myself constantly saying, 'I really need to go see that part of the state again.' I have always loved the Show-Me State, but age has made me appreciate it much more. I know that every state has unique characteristics, but ours is truly something special. We have the big cities along our eastern and western borders mirroring the national geography. We have mountainous areas to the south and west, and cotton fields in the southeast. We have wide-open plains to the north, and amazing rivers that run along some of the most beautiful parts of the state in between."

Amanda has made it her career to showcase the hidden gems, historically significant spots, and unique attractions of

• •

her adopted home to locals and visitors alike; she's convinced friends, family, and followers across the country that this Midwestern state that they might not have been able to find on a map is diverse, creative, and alluringly livable.

We really do have it all. If you want to have a metropolitan night out, look no further than the Central West End in St. Louis or the Power and Light District in Kansas City. If you want to enjoy historical downtown restaurants and walkable streets, check out Jefferson City, St. Charles, Cape Girardeau, or Branson. If you want to catch a college football game, you have Mizzou's Faurot Field, the campus of Missouri State, or even Division II powerhouse Northwest Missouri State.

World-changing history happened here, from the rising demands for equal human rights exerted by enslaved people at the courthouse in St. Louis to Winston Churchill's "Iron Curtain" speech in Fulton.

Our wonders both are natural and architectural. The Ozark Mountains, hundreds of caves, glades teeming with wildlife, and many fast, clear rivers and streams provide solace and strength that only wild spaces can give. And Missouri certainly rivals any state in the nation when it comes to beautiful, historic churches. These range from the Cathedral Basilica in St. Louis to the thousands of steeples you see dotting the rural hillsides as you travel. We have temples, mosques, churches, synagogues, houses of prayer, and Buddhist retreat centers for Missourians seeking peace and purpose.

• •

There is no doubt that Missouri has something for everyone. Maybe that's one of our "problems." We have so much to do, all within a couple of hours' drive, that often we take these things for granted. John once saw a poll of St. Louisans that showed that only about half of all people who call that city home have actually visited the Gateway Arch. We have one of the most iconic pieces of architecture in the world, yet often we pass it by without a second thought. It is our sincere hope that this book will get us excited about what Missouri has to offer.

2021 is our Bicentennial, so what better time than now to begin to check these things off your bucket list? You may be wondering how many of these 100 the authors actually have done. The honest answer is, most! But the few that we haven't, we plan to visit in the coming months. We want to cross all of these wonderful Missouri places off of our bucket lists while we still have time!

—John W. Brown and Amanda E. Doyle

Red's Giant Hamburg

FOOD AND DRINK

DRINK AND DISCOVER
ON THE MISSOURI SPIRITS
EXPEDITION (MSE)

Though our beer heritage is well-established and our wine cred extends way back, Missouri-distilled spirits still are on the upward climb for recognition. Enter the state Craft Distillers Guild: with a nod to the intrepid explorers Lewis and Clark, they've designated participating distillers as Missouri Spirits Exchange (MSE) Outfitters along a path that covers the entire state . . . and includes every sort of quaffable from gin and brandy to whiskey and amaro. Taste your way from west to east and north to south, and, along with your knowledge, expand your collection of stamps from each producer you visit. More stamps means more rewards and a wider range of choices when it's your turn to mix the cocktails! See the 33 (as of this printing) distillers and print your own expedition log at the website.

missouricraftdistillersguild.com/missouri-spirits-expedition

> ### TIP
> Venture to tiny Higbee, Missouri, with just 568 residents but two stops on the expedition (Skullsplitter Spirits and Woodsmen Distilling) and two long-standing, white oak barrel-makers.

● ●

BOTTOMS UP
AT BOULEVARD BREWING

One of the country's best-known (and highest-selling) craft brewers turns out its bottles from a funky, laid-back facility just outside downtown Kansas City. The original brewing building once served as the laundry for the Santa Fe railroad (check out how close the tracks are). While their pale ale and unfiltered wheat beers are the solid mainstays, Boulevard also pushes the envelope with the Smokestack series, including Tank 7 saison and Dark Truth imperial stout. Boulevard has branched out from beer into some of the market's fastest-growing segments, including Fling canned cocktails and Quirk spiked seltzer. As if great drinks weren't enough, business boomed enough to support the acquisition and rehab of an adjacent building that's known now as the Tours & Rec Center. Your brewery tours and tastings originate here, but there's also merch to peruse and an inviting fourth-floor party deck, with shuffleboard games and an open-air patio.

2534 Madison Ave., Kansas City
816-701-7247, boulevard.com

TIP
You can't swing a six-pack in this state without finding another micro-brewery. With more than 140 independent craft brewers in the state, there's bound to be a great one near you. Check mocraftbeer.com for a great list.

FOLLOW THE BEAN TO THE BAR
AT ASKINOSIE CHOCOLATE

Not many delicious enterprises begin when a criminal defense attorney has an epiphany while driving ... but this unique chocolatier never has been about a typical path. Founder Shawn Askinosie had literally prayed for a new career when he hit upon his golden ticket: make the most exquisite chocolate available, and learn everything about its history, its botanical and cultural underpinnings, and its economic and environmental backstory, to create a fair and sustainable business for himself and all the people involved in the supply chain. Today, the Springfield-based confectioner, which sources 100 percent of its cocoa beans directly from farmers, sells tons of award-winning chocolate and connects Missouri kids to their peers in places like Tanzania and Ecuador through its cultural exchange program, Chocolate University (funded by donations and factory tour admission). Shop their factory store or find Askinosie at retailers all over the state and beyond. Sweet!

514 E. Commercial St., Springfield
417-862-9900, askinosie.com

TIP
Chocolate's not just for dessert anymore! Check the recipes at askinosie.com/learn/recipes for ways to use their products, including a pumpkin-and-ricotta-filled cocoa ravioli.

CAN'T GET ENOUGH CHOCOLATE?

You might do a double-take when presented with a box of Christopher Elbow artisanal chocolates. With their glossy, painted finishes and faceted surfaces, you could hardly be faulted for thinking you're staring at a selection of precious jewels. And this confectioner backs up the shine with delicious substance—from fleur de sel caramels to fruit-infused ganache, these sweet bites delight with a wide array of flavor profiles. Christopher Elbow, the man himself, had a great career as a chef in Las Vegas and elsewhere before returning home to Kansas City to perfect the chocolate craft he came to serendipitously. Now, his boxed collections are one of the most coveted gifts in town.

Christopher Elbow Chocolates
1819 McGee St., Kansas City
816-842-1301, elbowchocolates.com

SAMPLE SEASONAL CUISINE
AT BLUESTEM

Longevity is not a common feature in the restaurant business, and remaining on "hip eatery" lists is even more rare. Colby and Megan Garrelts seem to have cracked the code, though, at their subtly chic Bluestem, in Kansas City's stylish Westport neighborhood since 2004. Thanks to his innovative cuisine and her fresh takes on desserts, both Garrelts and the restaurant have been nominated multiple times for James Beard Foundation honors. Yes, but what about the food? From heirloom tomato soup to a to a tender lamb ragu, the dinner menu sings with what's freshest now. Plenty of folks make a stop just for the thoughtful cocktails and tasty bar snacks, too.

900 Westport Rd., Kansas City
816-561-1101, bluestemkc.com

TIP
Chef Megan's always experimenting with the ice-cream maker, and recent flavors include Concord grape and sweet corn. You can grab a pint or two of ice cream to go!

DUTCH TREAT YOURSELF
AT VAN GOGH'S EETERIE

Well, it's Dutch fusion cuisine, for starters. Fused with what? Indonesian influences show up on the lunch and dinner menus in choices like shrimp *nasi goreng* (a fried rice dish), alongside the popular house-made sausages, fried salt cod, and other more traditional flavors. Their claim to fame, though, occupies an entire menu of its own: *pannenkoeken*, or Dutch pancakes. They come sweet, they come savory, and they come topped with everything from shawarma beef and pickled onions to apples, cinnamon, and caramel. There are plenty of vegan choices, too (and a dedicated, gluten-free, vegan fryer in the kitchen.) Throw in the city's first draft kombucha bar, and it's a unique destination for breakfast, lunch, or dinner.

334 E. Commercial St., Springfield
417-344-0085, vangoghseeterie.com

TIP
Yes, of course, there is a dish called Starry Night—a Dutch pancake with blueberries, berry compote, lemon-ginger drizzle, ice cream, and powdered sugar.

HAVE A SLICE TODAY
AT SHAKESPEARE'S PIZZA

As we're writing this entry, your faithful authors actually can conjure up the unmistakable smell of dough and sauce and cheese and magic that washes over us when we step inside the doors of Shakespeare's in downtown Columbia. Even though the original, 42-year home of the beloved pizza dive was demolished (and then rebuilt, with apartments on top), the new Shakespeare's on Ninth Street manages to be exactly what the people have always wanted. Stop by at lunch for a slice and a Coke, or make a dinner stop and enjoy the U-shaped "mafia booths" and a few pies with your friends. Grab a red napkin, give a nod to the "Liquor Guns & Ammo" sign, and dig in.

225 S. Ninth St., Columbia
573-449-2454, shakespeares.com

TIP
If you're passing through town and need to keep trucking, call ahead and pick up a half-bake to recreate the Shakespeare's magic in your home oven.

SEE WHY KANSAS CITY BBQ
IS FAMOUS

When people mention Kansas City barbecue, they can mean a lot of things, and it always causes a debate. But one thing that is not debatable is Arthur Bryant's status as one of the best of the best! When you have had Presidents Truman, Carter, and Obama in your restaurant, you must be doing something right. There is no question that there are numerous places to get barbecue in Kansas City, but your quest won't be complete without a stop in the joint that gets national attention year after year.

1727 Brooklyn Ave., Kansas City
816-231-1123, arthurbryantsbbq.com

BEER ME!
AT ANHEUSER-BUSCH

Been on the free Anheuser-Busch tour? If not, do that first and meet back here.

OK, now we're all caught up and ready for the premium experience. For $35, upgrade to the Beermaster Tour, which takes aficionados into the fermentation cellars, the historic Brew House, the Clydesdale Stable and Tack Room, a packaging/bottling line, and private VIP tasting room at tour's end. (If you're under 21, the tour drops to $15 and soft drinks; no one under 13 can enjoy this particular tour flavor, although there's plenty for kids to do on other tours.) You'll also get some nifty A-B swag to take home, including a Beermaster certificate of completion. How proud will your folks be to see that on your wall, next to any other earned diplomas?

1200 Lynch St., St. Louis

314-577-2626, budweisertours.com/locations/st-louis-missouri.html

PASSIONATE ABOUT THE PONIES?

If you're as taken with the pageantry and lore of the Anheuser-Busch brand as with the beer, another great stop is Warm Springs Ranch, the Clydesdale breeding farm that supplies all the iconic Clydesdales to the A-B breweries around the country. Guided walking tours of the facility include peeks at the veterinary suites, the hitch and harness storage (for the many promotional and parade appearances the spokeshorses make each year), and the plush travel trailers used to transport them in style and comfort. And, of course, there are plenty of chances to see these majestic animals up close.

Warm Springs Ranch
25270 State Hwy. 98, Boonville
888-972-5933, warmspringsranch.com

RAISE A GLASS
OF MISSOURI WINE

Whether you enjoy the sweet stuff that built our historical viticultural district's early reputation, or you want to try award-winning Nortons, Chambourcins, Chardonels, and other dry varietals, choose a reputable local vineyard and let them educate your palate. Here we're highlighting the four Cs of the Sainte Genevieve wine region, but by no means should you stop with these!

Cave Vineyard focuses on four native grape varieties, including the sweet, white Traminette. And yes, there is a for-real saltpeter cave underneath the tasting room, where guests are welcome to take their bottle purchases to enjoy. Just 15 minutes down the bucolic road, **Chaumette Vineyards & Winery** enjoys a scenic hilltop location for its tasting room, complete with gourmet dining, an onsite chapel, and a clutch of overnight villas for the full destination experience. Their dry rosé is a favorite! From the Chaumette property, it's a short, three-quarter-mile

---

TIP
Got beer drinkers in your group? It'll be OK! Charleville brews several great beers, including the popular Tornado Alley Amber Ale. Cave has a sideline label, S.I.L. Brews, operated by the family Sons-In-Law.

---

hike on a back trail to reach **Charleville Vineyard, Winery &
Brewery** and Microbrewery, where a rustic front porch view
of the wooded surroundings instantly lowers blood pressure.
Finally, check out the sprawling **Crown Valley Winery** complex
(which includes a brewery and distillery): a great place for your
party to while away the afternoon, enjoying everything from
crisp chardonel to the house-brewed Fizzy Izzy root beer.

Cave
21124 Cave Rd., Ste. Genevieve
573-543-5284, cavevineyard.com

Chaumette
24345 State Rd. WW, Ste. Genevieve
573-747-1000, chaumette.com

Charleville
16937 Boyd Rd., Ste. Genevieve
573-756-4537, charlevillevineyard.com

Crown Valley Winery
23589 State Rte. WW, Ste. Genevieve
866-207-9463, crownvalley.com

DO DINNER . . . AND SO MUCH MORE
AT TOP OF THE ROCK

Dinner at Top of the Rock is not just a meal; it's an experience. As a matter of fact, if you go to the restaurant expecting only to have a meal, you are underestimating the entire trip. It's best to go several hours early to make sure you have enough time to fit everything in. If you are lucky enough to have a dinner reservation around sunset, you get to hear the bagpipes playing as the cannon is loaded and shot, where it echoes through the hills. Then you get to enjoy a fantastic meal at one of several distinct restaurants on the property. Once the sun goes down, there is certainly no need to rush, as you can grab one last drink under the stars as Table Rock Lake goes quiet below.

190 Top of the Rock Rd., Ridgedale
417-335-2777, bigcedar.com/attractions/top-of-the-rock

TIP

Arrive about two hours early! You need to get there early enough to do the Lost Canyon Cave and Nature Trail Tour in an electric cart. Make sure you get the drinks at the cave bar! After the tour, you will then be shuttled to the restaurant, where you'll want to save enough time to tour the facility, including Arnie's General Store, and then go inside the Ancient Ozarks Natural History Museum.

ROLL ON IN
TO LAMBERT'S CAFE

If you've been to Lambert's Cafe, then you already know why people wait for hours just to get in. If you haven't been, then it's time to discover the legend of "throwed rolls." It all started back in 1942 at a small cafe on South Main Street in Sikeston that held only a few dozen people. Now, Lambert's has grown into massive eateries in three locations (two in Missouri), where the world-famous rolls are just the beginning of the fun. Those rolls are followed by skillet-sized entrées and family-style sides that are served right onto the table. The unique wall decorations also are something to behold, because you never know what you might see the next time you visit, or which famous customer you might be seated next to!

Lambert's Cafe—Sikeston
2305 E. Malone Ave., Sikeston
573-471-4261

Lambert's Cafe—Ozark
1800 W. State Hwy. J., Ozark
417-581-7655

throwedrolls.com

SCREAM
FOR MISSOURI ICE CREAM PARLORS

Ice cream and Missouri have a historic tradition that dates back to the 1904 World's Fair in St. Louis. And although everyone has their own favorite from their corner of the state, a few varieties have risen through the ranks to earn statewide, and even nationwide, attention. These are the ones that need to be on your ice cream bucket list.

Ted Drewes Frozen Custard in St. Louis has been named the World's Best Ice Cream, according to SoolNua's World Ice Cream Index Challenge, so there is certainly no argument about this one.

Kansas Citians seem divided on their rankings, although **Betty Rae's** and **Foo's** appeared in every ranking we could find, dating back several years.

In Springfield, it's all about **Andy's Frozen Custard**. Thankfully, Andy's has branched out to other cities (and states) at this point.

In Jefferson City, you have to visit the historic **Central Dairy Ice Cream Parlor,** just like generations of kids and adults have done.

teddrewes.com   eatandys.com

bettyraes.com   centraldairy.biz

GO BACK IN TIME
WITH RED'S GIANT HAMBURG

The very first drive-through restaurant in the country opened in Springfield way back in 1947, and became a legend along US Route 66. Red's Giant Hamburg closed in 1984 but came roaring back to life in 2019, bringing back a lot of nostalgia along with some great burgers. The location has changed, but the vibe and much of the menu remains as Red Chaney envisioned it when he expanded his Sinclair gas station to include a cafe. Even the historic sign that welcomed thousands of weary travelers along the "Mother Road" has been reproduced, and now stands as a beacon to a new generation of hungry motorists.

2301 W. Sunshine St., Springfield
417-865-7337, facebook.com/redshamburg

BE A WINNER
WITH CASHEW CHICKEN DINNER

Just what you'd expect near the middle of the great United States, right? An explosion of joints serving a Chinese culinary delight: cashew chicken. But the fact is, Springfield is the birthplace, heir, and rightful claimant to this crave-worthy concoction: chunks of deep-fried chicken in brown oyster sauce with green onions and halved cashews. Dozens of spots around town have it, or a variant, on the menu, and spots across the country feature "Springfield-style cashew chicken," but you'll want to hit up Leong's Asian Diner. It's owned by the next generation of Leongs after the dish's creator, David Leong, a Chinese immigrant, naturalized citizen, and Army veteran. Leong's own life story found its way into the 2014 documentary, *The Search for General Tso*.

1540 W. Republic Rd., Springfield
417-887-7500, leongsasiandiner.com

TIP
Don't miss another Leong family creation on the menu!
The crispy eggrolls use peanut butter as their secret ingredient.

REIMAGINE DESSERT
AT LA PATISSERIE CHOUQUETTE

Stepping through the door at La Patisserie Chouquette feels a bit like entering a high-end fashion boutique . . . an illusion that's furthered by the exquisite designer handbags and couture shoes gleaming in the glass cases. It might take you a moment to register that these are, in fact, couture cakes. Those colorful gems nestled under bright lights nearby? The shop's famous French macarons, in a wild assortment of flavors. It all makes the "regular" bakery items seem ordinary—until you taste them. The shop is the realm of pastry chef Simone Faure, whose childhood in New Orleans informs both her culinary directions and her embrace of St. Louis (another city with French roots and sensibilities). Her madeleines, croissants, and bourbon pecan sticky buns will knock your socks off.

1626 Tower Grove Ave., St. Louis
314-932-7935, simonefaure.com

TIP

Chef Simone is a sucker for an immersive theme, so if you can swing a visit during October, you'll be in the thick of Month of Magic, a Harry Potter-inspired extravaganza in which the shop is decked out and chocolate frogs, fizzing whizzbees, chocolate snitches, pumpkin pasties, and butterbeer fudge fill the shelves.

DINE LAKESIDE
AT JB HOOKS

There are dozens of restaurants at the Lake of the Ozarks that have amazing views, yet few are able to stand the test of time and remain top-notch, year after year. That's exactly why JB Hooks is a legendary establishment at the lake. Not only does the restaurant win culinary awards annually, the 14-mile views of Lake of the Ozarks are stunning as well. For nearly three decades, this has been the place to be—in a resort town, no less—and the views and the food keep getting better. And if you happen to be there when the powerboat races take place, you have a front row seat to all the action.

2260 Bagnell Dam Blvd., Lake Ozark
573-365-3255, jbhooks.com

OTHER LAKE OF THE OZARKS TOP VIEWS

Bentley's Pub
3100 Bagnell Dam Blvd., Lake Ozark
573-365-5301, bentleysrestaurantmo.com

Paradise Tropical Restaurant and Bar
430 Tropical Trails End Rd., Sunrise Beach
573-374-4777, paradisetropicalrestaurant.com

H. Toad's Bar & Grill
2325 Bittersweet Rd., Lake Ozark
573-365-5620, htoads.com

Dog Days Bar and Grill
1232 Jeffries Rd., Osage Beach
573-348-9797, dogdays.ws

Michael's Steak Chalet
1440 Swiss Village Rd., Osage Beach
573-348-3611, steakchalet.com

Backwater Jack's
4341 Beach Dr., Osage Beach
573-348-6639, backwaterjacks.com

Ruthie D's
4466 Horseshoe Bend Rd., Lake Ozark
573-964-6448, ruthiedsrestaurant.com

SHOP THE STALLS
OF SOULARD MARKET

Any place in business since 1779 must be doing at least a few things right: in this case, bringing together vendors of everything from fresh, organic produce to knockoff designer sunglasses. The mini-donuts alone will keep you moving while you ponder meats, cheeses, spices, baked goods . . . and maybe that pet bunny you've been considering. Grab flowers for your love or a St. Louis–themed gift basket for your hostess at this busy farmers market in the Soulard neighborhood, where it's been since early French colonists used the space to trade produce and livestock.

The real bargain here is the free people-watching. Saturday morning is the best bet for the street musicians and full experience of this covered marketplace. Fun architectural trivia: the building housing the shops of the Grand Hall was built in 1929, but is modeled on an Italian foundling hospital from 1419!

730 Carroll St., St. Louis
314-622-4180, soulardmarket.com

TIP
Get yourself a cocktail chaser to go with all that shopping: Julia's Market Café serves up a mean Bloody Mary and a credible beignet, too!

CHILL OUT
AT THE VENICE CAFÉ

Leave your cares (and your credit cards) behind, and enter the parallel relax-iverse that is the patio at the Venice Café. Part hippie hangout, part music venue, part psychedelic mosaic-and-mural party headquarters the Venice is a staple of St. Louis nightlife. You can tell a lot about a bar by how many industry folks are willing to spend their off-hours there—and here, the answer is, "a lot." The bathrooms—even the bathrooms!—have more personality than some other entire establishments. Stop by for the band, sample a drink from the cash-only bar, and see if you don't lose track of time.

1903 Pestalozzi St., St. Louis
314-772-5994, thevenicecafe.com

TIP
That visual mishmash on every conceivable surface is curated carefully by owner Jeff Lockheed. And your contribution is welcome! Deposit any artwork you wish to donate by the alley entrance for consideration . . . then come back and see if you can find it.

GO HIGH
AT A ROOFTOP RESTAURANT/BAR

One of the best trends re-emerging across the country is the proliferation of rooftop bars and restaurants, giving you the perfect view of the city or countryside. Thankfully, Missouri has plenty of locations that fit the bill. From a bar that looks right into Busch Stadium to a spot where folks gather at sundown to celebrate another day living and working among passionate and proud Springfieldians, these are perches you don't want to miss.

360
(see Busch Stadium from the bird's-eye view)
1 S. Broadway, St. Louis
314-241-8439, 360-stl.com

Rooftop Terrace Bar at Moonrise Hotel
(a giant kinetic moon sculpture marks the spot)
6117 Delmar Blvd., St. Louis
314-726-2222, moonrisehotel.com/food-drinks/eclipse-restaurant/

Angad Rooftop Terrace at Angad Arts Hotel
(unique indoor/outdoor spot overlooks
downtown skyline)
3550 Samuel Shepard Dr., St. Louis
314-561-0033, angadartshotel.com/dining-bars

Vin De Set
(the rooftop restaurant that started the revival in town)
2017 Chouteau Ave., St. Louis
314-241-8989, vindeset.com/

Percheron
(casual, festive spot with sweeping city views)
2101 Central St., Kansas City
866-531-2400, crossroadshotelkc.com/food-and-drink/
percheron-rooftop-bar

The Roof at The Broadway
(firepits, music, and drinks above Collegetown USA)
1111 E. Broadway, Columbia
573-875-7000, thebroadwaycolumbia.com/the-roof

The Well Bar Grill and Rooftop
(party spot above the Waldo neighborhood)
7421 Broadway, Kansas City
816-361-1700, waldowell.com

Vantage Rooftop Lounge and Conservatory
at Hotel Vandivort
(use the wooden mallet to strike the historic bell,
part of a sunset ritual observed each evening)
260 E. McDaniel St., Springfield
817-851-1768, rooftopvantage.com

Power and Light District

MUSIC AND ENTERTAINMENT

LIVE IT UP
ON THE BRANSON STRIP

The world-famous Branson Strip has changed a lot over the years. State Highway 76 has a bit of everything, from massive theaters to war memorials, buffet restaurants to thrilling roller coasters. But one thing is for sure: it's sure to be different each year you go!

One of the best new additions in recent years is the Branson Ferris Wheel. This 150-foot-tall wheel was famous long before it arrived in Branson. Chicago's Navy Pier Ferris Wheel previously lit up the Windy City for nearly 20 years. The Ferris Wheel is in an entertainment complex called the Track Family Fun Park, which also has high-rise go-kart tracks and other thrill rides.

The Branson Tracks
3335 W. 76 Country Blvd., Branson
417-334-1612, bransontracks.com

TIP
Development in Branson often seems to happen in waves along Highway 76. Right now, the "hot area" is along the stretch of the Strip near Highway 165. That's where another new addition, the Branson Aquarium on the Boardwalk, opened in 2020. It's best to find a place to park and venture out from there, since many attractions are within walking distance.

FEEL THE VIBE
AT THE AMERICAN JAZZ MUSEUM

Missouri is known for its jazz heritage, so it only makes sense that a museum that celebrates the iconic music genre resides in the Show-Me State. The American Jazz Museum is perfectly positioned at what is known at Kansas City's 18th and Vine District, which is recognized as one of the historical points of origin of jazz music. In fact, the museum itself has a jazz club on the premises that still provides live music several nights per week. This is less of a museum and more of a living, breathing clinic on what the spirit of jazz is all about.

1616 E. 18th St., Kansas City
816-474-8463, americanjazzmuseum.org

TASTE THE SAWDUST
AT CIRCUS FLORA

It's worth starting a summer circus tradition with your family and friends, and there's no better place than at the charming, one-ring wonder under a classic, red-and-white-striped big top in the Grand Center Arts District of St. Louis. For nearly a month, a mundane parking lot utterly is transformed by high-wire daredevils, aerialists, jugglers, acrobats, fast-paced and funny animal acts, and irrepressible clowns. It's a circus in the style of classical, European troupes, with generations of family performers and an emphasis on skills and substance over gaudy glitz. You can sit close enough to have sawdust from the pounding horses' hooves fly in your lap, if that's your thing. Live music makes the experience even more magical, and the very personal touch lasts all the way through the exit, when you can meet and talk to all the performers as you leave the tent.

3401 Washington Blvd., St. Louis
314-827-3830, circusflora.org

WATCH THE WORLD
AT THE ST. LOUIS INTERNATIONAL FILM FESTIVAL

Bright lights, red carpet . . . is this Hollywood? Nope, because even with the star power and great movie premieres, parking is way cheaper! That's the scene at the film festival that takes over screens throughout St. Louis for two weeks each November. The best in features, shorts, documentaries, and experimental film from around the globe are accessed as easily as falling off a log and into a plush theater seat. It's also an excellent venue for showcasing top homegrown talent, with lots of screen time and promotion devoted to Missouri-written/made/inspired/connected movies. Panels, discussions, parties, and prizes round out the schedule. And the presenting nonprofit organization, Cinema St. Louis, offers a plethora of cinematic events year-round, from the LGBTQ-focused QFest to the St. Louis Filmmakers Showcase (SLIFF).

314-289-4151, cinemastlouis.org

TIP
SLIFF isn't the only show in the business! Pop over to Columbia for the True/False Film Fest, which takes over the town with nonfiction cinema, art, music, and some serious madcap fun. truefalse.org

GET THE BLUES
INSIDE THE ROUND BARN
IN KIRKSVILLE

Perhaps one of the more interesting music venues in the entire state, the Round Barn is a classic spot to hear blues music in a truly unique way. The old barn was built back in 1913, mainly to hold hay and other farm implements, and it has stood the test of time—even landing on the National Historic Register in 2001. The owner decided a few years ago to convert it into a music venue. Since the refurbishment, some of the best blues artists from across the country have come to this farm outside of Kirksville to play for thousands of fans in a round barn that stands 64 feet wide and 64 feet high. So, if you want to see a concert in a way that few can claim, this is the way to do it.

2313 State Hwy. P, Kirksville
660-665-2760, facebook.com/RoundBarnBlues

HURT SO GOOD
AT THE NATIONAL BLUES MUSEUM

Though it hasn't blown its own horn as much as some other iconic music towns (think Chicago, Nashville, and the like), St. Louis made a major move to claim its own place in American musical history with the 2016 opening of the National Blues Museum. The slick, interactive facility celebrates the influence of blues music on American and international culture: from the cotton fields of the South to the Great Migration, from the early days of radio to live concerts produced right in the museum's own venue, visitors see and hear the story of the blues from the beginning to today's torch-bearers. The complex history of this most homegrown of genres, as well as its influence on the jazz/folk/rap/country/rock music of today, comes to life here with incredible historic photographs, cool musical artifacts, and hands-on music-making opportunities.

615 Washington Ave., St. Louis
314-925-0016, nationalbluesmuseum.org

TIP
Don't miss the series of stations throughout the museum that let you mix guitar, piano, and other tracks to create your own blues masterpiece . . . and then emails you the final creation.

CATCH THE INCREDIBLE DOG CHALLENGE
AT PURINA FARMS

Purina Farms in Gray Summit is one of the most fun places in Missouri to see why humans and our four-legged friends have gotten along so well over the years. You'll get to watch some of the most talented pooches in the world perform their tricks inside the Incredible Dog Arena. You also can see some breeds put their best paws forward during the world-class dog shows at the Purina Event Center. There even is an area where you can get up close and personal with the domestic farm animals. But the trip to the farm takes on added interest during the annual Incredible Dog Challenge, when the most talented animals on the planet take part in a skills challenge that is broadcast on network television.

500 William Danforth Way, Gray Summit
314-982-3232, purina.com/about-purina/purina-farms

GET ENERGIZED
IN THE POWER AND LIGHT DISTRICT

The hottest new entertainment district in the entire Midwest sits in downtown Kansas City and has become both the go-to spot for daytime getaways and the hot spot for nightlife. If you ever wanted to get that big-city feel right here in the Show-Me State, this is THE place to do it. The Power and Light District has a little bit of something for everybody. Along with cool restaurants and hip boutique stores, you also have some of the best concert venues for the hottest artists on the planet to entertain their fans. Some people like the vibe so much, they have decided to move into the luxury apartments in the district so they can live the big-city lifestyle every day!

50 E. 13th St., Ste. 200, Kansas City
816-842-1045, powerandlightdistrict.com

TIP
If you want to see the Power and Light District at its best, find a day or night when there is a Chiefs or Royals game taking place, along with a concert at one of the venues. The place is electric! There are dozens of dining options to choose from and many hotels within walking distance.

EXPERIENCE AN EVENING
AT THE KAUFFMAN CENTER FOR THE PERFORMING ARTS

The Kauffman Center for the Performing Arts hosts some of the most amazing performances every while while also being one of the most impressive structures you will ever see. When you put those two factors together, you really need to be inside to experience what it's like to see and hear a performance live. The Center opened in 2011 and has been getting rave reviews ever since. It is the home of the Kansas City Symphony, the Lyric Opera of Kansas City, and the Kansas City Ballet. A performance by any of those is a treat, but if you are trying to decide what to put on your bucket list, make sure you see the annual tradition of the Kansas City Ballet's performance of *The Nutcracker*. There is no better way to kick off the holidays.

Kauffman Center for the Performing Arts
1601 Broadway Blvd., Kansas City
816-994-7222, kauffmancenter.org

Kansas City Ballet
500 W. Pershing Rd., Kansas City
816-931-2232, kcballet.org

Lyric Opera of Kansas City
1725 Holmes St., Kansas City
816-471-4933, kcopera.org

CATCH A LIVE CONCERT
UNDER THE STARS

Perhaps the only thing better than listening to your favorite music live and in-person is listening to that music under the stars. Starlight Theatre in Kansas City is the perfect spot to hear the biggest artists and bands currently touring the country, enjoy Broadway shows, and even see smaller productions. This iconic venue at Swope Park has been around since 1951, but continues to reinvent itself with all-encompassing events, and now offers pre-show entertainment and dinner on-site. They even have found a way to beat the elements by opening a small, indoor venue to keep the shows going year-round.

4600 Starlight Rd., Kansas City
816-363-7827, kcstarlight.com

TIP

In St. Louis, you have the Muny. It is billed as America's oldest and largest outdoor amphitheater. A night at the Muny has been a tradition in Forest Park for families since 1917. On show night, you can get to the park early and see hundreds of people tailgating with wine and cheese or other delicacies, prior to the opening curtain.

The Muny
1 Theatre Dr., St. Louis
314-361-1900, muny.org

RETURN TO THE RAGTIME
OF SCOTT JOPLIN

It was the dawn of a new century, and spirits were high. The bouncy syncopations of a new, "ragged" style of piano music were innovated and popularized by no one more than Missouri transplant Scott Joplin. He played violin and cornet, sang, and composed operas as well, but lively rags like "The Entertainer" and "The Maple Leaf Rag" were the hits the public demanded. Sedalia, his home in the late 1800s, now hosts the renowned Scott Joplin International Ragtime Festival each summer. Swinging band performances, period fashion shows, academic symposia, and much more mark these freewheeling days of music and fun.

660-826-2271, scottjoplin.org

TIP
If you're in town when it's not festival time, stop into the historic Katy Depot, where you can score Joplin-themed merchandise and recordings of some of the many acts who've performed in years past.

Katy Depot
600 E. Third St., Sedalia
660-826-2932, katydepotsedalia.com

GET DOWN HOME
AT THE MOUNTAIN MUSIC FESTIVAL

Don't tell anyone we told you, but the Arcadia Valley is about the prettiest part of this great state. And the Arcadia Valley Mountain Music Festival (which happens in May and October) is an appropriate way to spend some time in the Ozarks to enjoy it all. The festival showcases traditional country, bluegrass, and gospel music, with live bands over a couple of days on the grounds of the Ironton Courthouse. A small vendor area and carnival food booths keep you fed and watered, and if you feel like getting up to clog, two-step, or otherwise shake a leg, nobody's going to stop you! We recommend you bring your own chair for the courthouse lawn. And if you can make it to the October festival date, the Arcadia Valley High School parade on Saturday is packed with small-town charm, politicians in convertibles, impressive student-built floats . . . and candy, so much candy.

250 S. Main St., Ironton
314-517-4445, mountainmusicfestival.net

TIP
Take some of the region home with you in the form of custom-blended, handmade soaps from the Arcadia Valley Soap Company, across the street. We love the Tiger Pride lemongrass scent!

Arrowhead Stadium

SPORTS AND RECREATION

HIKE
ELEPHANT ROCKS STATE PARK

It took the earth about 1.5 billion years to create these strange geological rock formations, so you can bet it's worth your time to drive to Iron County to see what the hype is all about. It's hard to put into words what Elephant Rocks State Park is all about, but it's also hard to forget. These massive granite boulders look like they were placed on top of mountains, almost as though giants placed them there as toys a long time ago. Some of the round boulders are nearly 30 feet tall and more than 34 feet wide. Etchings remain visible from when miners worked on these stones more than 100 years ago. The walking path gives you a great view of some geological formations that, likely, you won't see anywhere else in the world.

7390, 7406 State Hwy. 21, Belleview
573-697-5395, mostateparks.com/park/elephant-rocks-state-park

TIP

Make a day of it and do the trifecta! Johnson's Shut-Ins State Park and Taum Sauk Mountain State Park are just a few miles away. So, in one day you can see the prehistoric rock formations, one of the most interesting river rapids at the Shut-Ins, and the tallest point in Missouri in one short drive.

Johnson's Shut Ins
148 Taum Sauk Trl., Middle Brook
573-546-2450, mostateparks.com/park/johnsons-shut-ins-state-park

Taum Sauk Mountain State Park
State Hwy. CC, Ironton
573-546-2450, mostateparks.com/park/taum-sauk-mountain-state-park

GO INTO THE DEPTHS
OF THE BONNE TERRE MINE

When miners began excavating lead from beneath Bonne Terre, little did they know it would eventually be considered one of the best places to scuba dive in the country. The St. Joe Lead Company halted operations in the early 1960s in the mine, which over time filled with crystal-clear water. It now has become an amazing cave tour, and a top freshwater scuba diving venue.

If you want only the "deep earth tour," the trip still is a blast. The one-hour walking tour with a knowledgeable guide shows the history of the mine as you walk the mule trails. You will go deep into the earth, where it is a comfortable 65 degrees year-round. When you reach the water level, you can take the boat tour (which is highly recommended), so you can get a full understanding of what life was like for the miners in the late 1800s in the Iron Belt of Missouri.

If you are diving, you will be shocked at how clear the 58-degree water really is. Abundant lighting helps you see more than 100 feet below. There are very few places in the Midwest where you can do this type of deep-earth diving. It's so amazing that even *National Geographic* calls it "one of America's Top 10 Greatest Adventures."

185 Park Ave., Bonne Terre
888-843-3483, bonneterremine.com

VISIT OUR LEGENDS
AT THE MISSOURI SPORTS HALL OF FAME

If you are a fan of Missouri sports, there is one place that must be on your bucket list. The Missouri Sports Hall of Fame has all of our legends in one place, from high school to college to the pros. This museum, west of Springfield, is an amazing collection of the best of the best who have called the Show-Me State their home over the years. But it's more than just displays of the athletes and their memorabilia. You can see what it's like to compete at their level . . . and even against them! The interactive exhibits allow you to see what it's like to step up to the plate and face a Major League pitch or drive a NASCAR car.

3861 E. Stan Musial Dr., Springfield
417-889-3100, mosportshalloffame.com

HOOP IT UP
AT THE COLLEGE BASKETBALL EXPERIENCE

If you are a die-hard college basketball fan, the College Basketball Experience in downtown Kansas City is a destination that must be on your bucket list. As you will discover, this is not a museum; this is an experience, just as the name implies. Sure, there are plenty of exhibits where you can read about the history of the sport and the greats who have played and molded the game over the years. That includes the National Collegiate Basketball Hall of Fame, which opened in 2007. But this 41,500-square-foot, interactive facility is designed to allow basketball fans to "live" the game. When top college coaches and former players say there is nothing else like this in the world, take their word for it and check it out yourself.

1401 Grand Blvd., Kansas City
816-949-7500, collegebasketballexperience.com

OTHER "MUST SEE HOOPS" EVENTS

Missouri State Lady Bears

The hottest ticket at Missouri State University typically is the WOMEN's basketball team. The Lady Bears have been a perennial powerhouse, even making the NCAA Sweet Sixteen four times and the Final Four in 1992 and 2001.

Arch Madness

College basketball doesn't get much better than the annual Missouri Valley Conference Tournament that takes place in downtown St. Louis every March, better known as Arch Madness. It kicks off the excitement of the NCAA basketball tournament, as the Arch Madness Champion is assured a trip to the Big Dance.

Bass Pro Shops "Tournament of Champions"

One of the top high school basketball events in the country, this tourney brings in stars before they are stars! More than 60 players in this tournament have gone on to the NBA.

SPEND SATURDAY
AT A MIZZOU FOOTBALL GAME

Saturdays at Ol' Mizzou: there is nothing quite like it. The massive tailgate party prior to the event in Columbia is an event unto itself. The smell of barbecue wafting through the air, the sounds of laughter among the RVs, and the students making their way from the University of Missouri campus to Faurot Field are magical. The game itself is just one part of the event. Another is the lush, green field, the students sitting on the M in the north end zone, and the constant chant back and forth as "M-I-Z" hails from one side and "Z-O-U" echoes back from the other. And after the game, the party really begins. Students and alumni flood downtown Columbia to take part in a celebration that is truly second to none.

1 Champions Dr., Columbia
800-CAT-PAWS, mutigers.com

TIP
If you really want to make the experience complete, attend the annual homecoming game. Why is that such a big deal? The first known homecoming game ever was held in Missouri at Rollins Field on November 25, 1911 against the Kansas Jayhawks.

MORE COLLEGE ACTION

For more college action, grab a seat at the next Northwest Missouri State University football game in Maryville. Over the past few decades, the Bearcats have appeared in nine national championship games in NCAA Division II. They have won six of those national championships, making the team one of the most successful NCAA football teams in history. The stadium holds 6,500 fans, so it's an intimate environment, full of passionate and knowledgeable football fans who aren't used to seeing the home team lose very often, either!

Northwest Missouri State University Athletics
800 University Dr., Maryville
bearcatsports.com

ESCAPE
TO THE FUGITIVE BEACH

One of the more unusual swimming locations in the state is located near Rolla, in what feels like a Caribbean destination. The Fugitive Beach has beautiful turquoise waters, sandy beaches, and plenty of activities to make you feel like you truly have gone on vacation. This beach actually is an old quarry that has been transformed into the coolest swimming hole you can imagine. It has tiki bars, rental cabanas, and cushioned chairs, 20-foot-tall cliffs that you can jump from, and plenty of safety devices to keep everyone safe. It's hard to believe a place this tropical exists right off of Interstate 44, but if you are looking for a spot to beat the summer heat, it might be time to escape to the Fugitive Beach.

16875 County Rd. 5285, Rolla
fugitive-beach.com

EXPERIENCE A REBIRTH
AT ECHO BLUFF STATE PARK

First and foremost, there are a lot of people who don't want you to know about Echo Bluff! This 476-acre, hidden gem near Eminence has been known for years as a great place to get away from it all to experience towering bluffs, pristine creeks and rivers, open-air concerts, remote camping . . . and some other, less-wholesome, activities. The area used to be home to Camp Zoe, which operated from the 1920s until the late 1980s. After that, parts of the land became a party zone, where concerts deep in the woods took place, along with open drug use. So, the land was confiscated and sold to the state. As a result, Echo Bluff became Missouri's newest state park in 2016. Now, you can experience this amazing place for yourself, with modern cabins, dining options, and up-to-date amenities to go along with the nature.

34489 Echo Bluff Dr., Eminence
855-999-6980, mostateparks.com/park/echo-bluff-state-park

TAKE A HIKE
AT HA HA TONKA

One of the most picturesque hikes in the Show-Me State sits high on the bluffs above Lake of the Ozarks, near Camdenton. When you see how beautiful the Ozark Mountains are in this area, you understand why Robert McClure Snyder decided to build his "dream castle" in that location. Sadly, tragedy struck the family several times, including Snyder's death in one of the first fatal car accidents in history, and later the fire that destroyed the European-style mansion. The state park that remains open to the public today is a sight to behold. There are 12 official hiking trails, several natural bridges, caves, springs, and, of course, the castle ruins to see.

1491 State Rte. D, Camdenton
573-346-2986, mostateparks.com/park/ha-ha-tonka-state-park

CHECK OUT THE "LITTLE GRAND CANYON"

Grand Gulf State Park in the southern part of the state truly is a geological wonder. It actually is a collapsed cave system that has been exposed to sunlight, and now provides a spectacular hiking and sightseeing experience. The walls of the cavern are 130 feet from the base and stretch for nearly a mile, which must be seen to be put into perspective. The 250-foot-long natural bridge also is a must-see.

Grand Gulf State Park
State Hwy. W., Koshkonong
417-264-7600, mostateparks.com/park/grand-gulf-state-park

FLOAT
A MISSOURI STREAM

Summer in Missouri is a time when people get outside and into the water. For many people, that means float trips, and some of the finest floating rivers in the country can be found in the southern parts of the state. In fact, the Ozark National Scenic Riverways became the first designated national park for the preservation of a wild river system.

The Jacks Fork River between Alley Spring and Eminence is perfect any time of year. On the Current River, the best (and quietest) floats are above Big Spring, with several options to choose from, depending on what you are looking for. If you want to do the Eleven Point River through the Mark Twain National Forest, check out establishments that get you near Greer Spring, which is magical. If you are closer to mid-Missouri, you can't go wrong floating the Huzzah River at Huzzah Valley Resort near Steelville.

TIP
Most roads into prime floating territory lead off Interstate 44. If you're in the vicinity, it's worth a stop in Cuba to check out the colorful murals throughout downtown, commissioned to mark the town's 150th anniversary in 2007.

cubamomurals.com

MAKE THE DRIVE
TO DOGWOOD CANYON NATURE PARK

There are some places in Missouri that are just too beautiful for words. When you are talking about crystal-clear streams, towering waterfalls, peaceful meadows, and unspoiled wilderness, the only words for it are Dogwood Canyon. Nestled in the Ozark hills near the Arkansas border, this little slice of paradise is a nature lover's dream come true. Johnny Morris of Bass Pro Shops fame took what was already a beautiful valley and transformed it into something magical. Whether you do it by tram, foot, bike, or Jeep, this is one stretch of Missouri wilderness you simply cannot miss.

2038 W. State Hwy. 86, Lampe
877-459-5687, dogwoodcanyon.org

TIP
Once you are done with the tour, you MUST make time for lunch at the Canyon Grill. Not only is the food amazing, but you also get to dine next to one of the tallest waterfalls in the state of Missouri.

MAKE A PILGRIMAGE
TO THE GOLF MECCA
IN THE OZARK MOUNTAINS

Bass Pro Shops's owner, Johnny Morris, has made it a quest to develop a golf destination that rivals anything you will find in the world. He started with Top of the Rock, just south of Branson, and took off from there. He since has developed four additional courses in the Ozark Mountains, all next to each other. Some of these courses already have been showcased on the PGA Tour, and you can expect to see plenty more as the popularity of the courses grows.

Buffalo Ridge Spring was designed by Tom Fazio and has been rated the number one public golf course in Missouri by *Golf Magazine*. The spectacular views of the Ozark Mountains are made even more unique by the grazing bison on nearby prairies.

Mountain Top may be one of the most spectacular courses you will play anywhere in America. The 13-hole short course is cut through the Ozark Mountains, as designed by World Golf Hall of Famer Gary Player. Odds are, you will be marveling at the 300-million-year-old limestone rock formations as much as the perfectly manicured course.

Ozarks National is so good it has to be seen, and played, to be believed. Seeing it on TV during the Charles Schwab Series golf tournament on The Golf Channel was amazing, so it's hard to believe that it's even better in person. The course was designed by Bill Coore and Ben Crenshaw, and they took everything that nature provided and made it even better. There even is a 400-foot wooden bridge that connects the tee box and fairway of the 13th hole that is 60 feet above a creek. It's one thing to see this masterpiece in pictures; it's another to experience it in person.

Payne's Valley is the newest of the Johnny Morris courses, and the first public-access course designed by Tiger Woods, so you know it has to be special. The course is named in honor of Missouri legend Payne Stewart, who grew up about 45 miles away from this masterpiece. You can imagine, when one of the greatest golfers in history teams up with one of the greatest environmental visionaries of all time, the result is a course that rivals anything you will find, anywhere on the planet.

bigcedar.com/golf

OTHER COURSES IN MISSOURI YOU MUST HIT

Everybody has their favorite course, and it's hard to pick just a few great courses in Missouri that everyone needs to play. So we combed the rankings from *Golf Digest*, *Golf Magazine*, *Golf Advisor*, and other sites to see which ones were routinely ranked as a "top public golf course" in Missouri. Here is a good list to get you started.

Innsbrook Country Club Golf Course
596 Aspen Way Dr., Innsbrook
innsbrook-resort.com/golf

Old Kinderhook
678 Old Kinderhook Dr., Camdenton
oldkinderhook.com

The Missouri Bluffs Golf Club
18 Research Park Cir., St Charles
mobluffs.com

Stone Canyon Golf Club
22415 E. 39th St. S., Blue Springs
stonecanyongolfclub.com

The Lodge of the Four Seasons
315 Four Seasons Dr., Lake Ozark
4seasonsresort.com

Shoal Creek
8905 Shoal Creek Pkwy., Kansas City
shoalcreekgolf.com

Mozingo Lake Recreation Park Golf Course
25055 Liberty Rd., Maryville
mozingolake.com/

Osage National Golf Club
400 County Rd. 54-52, Lake Ozark
osagenational.com

Rolling Hills Country Club
13986 Country Club Rd., Versailles
rollinghillsozark.com

Sun Valley Golf Course
192 State Hwy. W., Elsberry
sunvalleygc.com

Ledgestone Golf Course
1600 Ledgestone Way, Reeds Spring
ledgestonegolf.com

ATTEND
A KANSAS CITY CHIEFS PLAYOFF GAME

There is no better environment for an NFL playoff football game than Arrowhead Stadium in Kansas City (unless you are playing for the opposing team.) And, judging by the way the Chiefs have played over the past few years, the odds of getting to see a playoff game in Kansas City are pretty good in the near future, as well. Arrowhead Stadium holds more than 76,000 fans, making it the sixth-largest NFL stadium in the country, even though Kansas City ranks 30th among the largest metro areas in the country. Although it is a legendary experience to see the Chiefs play in a playoff game, any game during the regular season ranks pretty high on the list of cool experiences.

One Arrowhead Dr., Kansas City
816-920-9300, chiefs.com

TIP
Keep in mind that playoff games in Kansas City typically take place in December, so it will be cold in the open-air stadium. And if you participate in the event like the locals, you will have to get to the stadium several hours early to take part in one of the most epic tailgating environments you will witness anywhere.

DO SOMETHING FISHY
AT BENNETT SPRING

For a lot of families in Missouri, you don't have to tell them twice to grab a rod and reel and go fishing. But on one particular day each and every year, it's almost like a holiday. Opening day of trout season at Bennett Spring State Park in Lebanon is a spectacle to behold. The anglers begin their trek early on March 1. Sure, it may be cold, and the traffic lines may be long to get into the park, but that's a part of the tradition. Long before the sun comes up, they put on their waders and begin walking into the frigid water, where they stand side by side as the water rushes by. As soon as the siren wails, the lines start flying into the water. Even if you don't like fishing, it truly is a sight to see.

26250 State Hwy. 64A, Lebanon
417-532-4338, mostateparks.com/park/bennett-spring-state-park

---

TIP
It's a similar scene on opening day of trout season at Meramec Spring Park, just south of St. James.

Meramec Spring Park
21880 Meramec Spring Dr., St James
573-265-7124, meramecspringpark.com

TAKE IN OPENING DAY
FOR THE ST. LOUIS CARDINALS

There is something magical about the Cardinals' opening day in downtown St. Louis. Typically, it happens in early April and is considered an unofficial holiday for the city. Even though the stadium holds about 45,000 fans, several hundred thousand spectators dressed in red descend on downtown St. Louis prior to the first home game. Maybe it's the fact that warmer weather is on the way, or the excitement that comes with all the hope of a new season, or maybe it's the generations of fans bonding in one small area, but truly you have to experience this event once to understand the lore. And once you do it one time, there is a good chance it will be on your annual pilgrimage list to usher in another year of the Birds on the Bat.

700 Clark St., St. Louis
314-345-9600, cardinals.com

TIP
The day begins with a citywide tailgate party at establishments near Busch Stadium, especially in the newly built Ballpark Village. People without tickets are glued to jumbo TVs across downtown showcasing the event. And once the game is over, few people leave quickly, as the party lasts well into the night.

CROSS-STATE TIP

The Kansas City Royals also put on quite a show for opening day. Kauffman Stadium is one of the most beautiful ballparks in the country, and there is no better place to spend an afternoon or evening.

Kansas City Royals
One Royal Way, Kansas City
816-921-8000, royals.com

RUN
A MISSOURI MARATHON

There are several major marathons in Missouri each year, all across the state. Some are themed events, and some are qualifiers for the Boston Marathon. So, if you are willing to put in the months of pounding the pavement early in the morning through the heat of the summer and the cold of Missouri winters, then there is a race for you to check off your bucket list. Here are some of the most popular annual races across Missouri.

MO Cowbell: St. Charles

This may be one of the most unique races you will ever run. The name says it all! Before you ever start running, you have a sing-along, or, shall we say, "cowbell-along." Then you run along the historic St. Charles riverfront, through the unique village of New Town, across the Missouri River, and along the Katy Trail.

mocowbellmarathon.com

GO! St. Louis Marathon: St. Louis

This marathon takes you across the bridges between Missouri and Illinois, past the Gateway Arch, Union Station, Busch Stadium, and the Anheuser-Busch Brewery. If you always have wanted to see the historic sights of St. Louis from the ground as you run, this is run for you.

gostlouis.org

• •

Kansas City Marathon: Kansas City

The Kansas City Marathon routinely has been one of the largest marathons in the state, dating back to 1979. It is run in October, which typically provides perfect running weather conditions in the Midwest. In this race, runners typically start at Crown Center and get to see all the great sights around the city, including Westport, the Plaza, and many of the fountains that have made Kansas City famous.

sportkc.org/marathon

Heart of America Marathon: Columbia

A Labor Day tradition since 1960, this mid-Missouri marathon will test your fitness, thanks to some picturesque, rolling hills along the course. The course also encompases long stretches of the Katy Trail and beautiful stretches throughout the Columbia area.

columbiatrackclub.com/hoa

Bass Pro Shops Conservation Marathon: Springfield

This Boston Marathon-qualifying event takes you through the streets of Springfield and past some of the attractions that make the Ozarks unique. You will pass the campus of Missouri State University and historic downtown Springfield while running on old Route 66, and you'll see the Wonders of Wildlife Museum and Aquarium and, of course, Bass Pro Shops.

fitness.basspro.com

• •

BIKE
THE KATY TRAIL

Most everyone knows about the Katy Trail at this point. What you may not know is how special it is. The Katy Trail is a unique treasure for Missouri, and there are some ways to do it right. The Katy Trail now is the country's longest recreational trail, running a grand total of 240 miles—nearly from border to border—across the state. It takes you past some of the most amazing sights you will see in all of Missouri. Whether it's around Rocheport, St. Charles, Augusta, Sedalia, or anyplace in between, you always will see something new, and always something special. New cafes and brewpubs are popping up along the trail as well, which are drawing more people to the trail and adding more energy to the already popular statewide attraction.

mostateparks.com/park/katy-trail-state-park

CHILL OUT
WITH THE ST. LOUIS BLUES

It's one thing to watch a hockey game on TV, but it's something entirely different to watch it in person. Of all the professional sports, hockey may offer the biggest difference between watching in person versus at home or at a bar. And when it comes to the St. Louis Blues, the home team fans are a notch above anything you have ever seen—or heard—before. There is no feeling on earth like the excitement of 20,000 screaming fans when a goal is scored, the sirens blast, and the laser light show illuminates the arena. The Gateway City waited 50 years for its team to win the Stanley Cup in 2019, so the fan base is stronger than ever. If you want to see professional hockey like it's meant to be played, just put on your blue and yellow Blue Note gear and follow the most passionate fans on the planet toward the Enterprise Center in downtown St. Louis.

1401 Clark Ave., St. Louis
314-622-BLUE, stlblues.com

SEE WHY
MISSOURI IS KNOWN AS THE "CAVE STATE"

There are over 6,000 explored caves within the state, giving Missouri the moniker of "the Cave State." So, it really should be on your list to explore at least a few of these natural wonders, especially since we live in such close proximity to so many. Although most of the 6,000 caves are inaccessible, many of these underground wonders are big enough, and safe enough, for us to enjoy.

Bridal Cave got its name thanks to the legend of the marriage of a Native American couple inside the cave many centuries ago inside the mammoth cave. In fact, many weddings still take place at the cave near the Lake of the Ozarks.

Meramec Caverns, near Stanton, has been a shelter for many people over the years, including Native Americans, French Colonial miners, and even Jesse James. It is one of the world's largest cave formations and has a unique feature known as the Stage Curtain. There also is an underground river, along with a "Wine Table" and a "seven-story mansion."

Fantastic Caverns near Springfield is more than just a cave: it's actually a system of caves so large that you need to take a tram tour to see it all. This cave network even has been used for concert venues, and was a speakeasy back during Prohibition.

Mark Twain Cave is the original cave attraction in Missouri, as it was made famous through the writings of the legendary author. Located just outside of Hannibal, the cave takes about 60 minutes to tour and gives you some insight into Twain's life. There

• •

even is a separate tour of Cameron Cave, which requires lanterns and takes you back in time to experience what cave exploration was like when Cameron first was discovered in the early 1900s.

Marvel Cave actually is part of Silver Dollar City, but is an attraction unto itself. It is one of the largest caves in the world, and has what is believed to be the largest cave entrance in the country. The entrance, which is known as the Cathedral Room, is more than 205 feet high, 225 feet wide, and 411 feet long. To give you an idea of how big that is, as the tour guide will tell you, they once inflated several hot air balloons inside that room. There are some tight squeezes along the path as you descend into one of the deepest caves in Missouri, but it is well worth the visit the next time you are in Branson.

Bridal
526 Bridal Cave Rd., Camdenton
573-346-2676, bridalcave.com

Fantastic
4872 N. Farm Rd. 125, Springfield
417-833-2010, fantasticcaverns.com

Meramec
1135 State Hwy. W., Sullivan
573-468-2283, americascave.com

Mark Twain
300 Cave Hollow Rd., Hannibal
573-221-1656, marktwaincave.com

Marvel
399 Silver Dollar City Pkwy., Branson
417-336-7100, facebook.com/MarvelCaveBranson

OTHER CAVES TO EXPLORE
Current River Cavern (Van Buren), Fisher Cave at Meramec State Park (Sullivan), Onondaga Cave (Leasburg), and Talking Rocks Cavern (Branson West)

• •

World War I Museum

CULTURE AND HISTORY

CHECK OUT
AMERICA'S BEST THEME PARK

Silver Dollar City has transformed itself over the past few years into a world-class attraction, even being named "America's Best Theme Park" by *USA Today*. Yes, the park has remained true to its theme celebrating the 1880s Ozark Mountains lifestyle, but if you haven't been lately, you truly have no idea what they have created in those mountains! Roller coaster engineers have crafted world-renowned rides like Outlaw Run, Time Traveler, and Wildfire, that roller coaster enthusiasts from around the world are flocking to experience. Make no mistake: if you want to see the classic shows and have some down-home cooking, you still can do that. If you also want to experience some of the highest-level thrill rides on the planet, look no further than Branson.

399 Silver Dollar City Pkwy., Branson
800-888-7277, silverdollarcity.com

OTHER MAJOR THEME PARKS
Six Flags St. Louis
4900 Six Flags Rd.,
Eureka
636-938-5300, sixflags.com/stlouis

Worlds of Fun
4545 Worlds of Fun Ave.,
Kansas City
816-454-4545, worldsoffun.com

GO UNDER THE SEA
AT WONDERS OF WILDLIFE

Wonders of Wildlife is one of the best aquariums you will see anywhere in the country, and you have only to travel to Springfield. Recognized by the readers of *USA Today* as "America's Best Aquarium," this massive underwater adventure offers more than 1.5 miles of immersive trails to explore. Take a journey through the planet's most exciting ecosystems, including the Open Ocean, Great Barrier Reef, Swamp at Night, and Amazon Rainforest, and meet more than 35,000 live animals along the way. Many cities have added aquariums in recent years, including St. Louis and Kansas City, and Wonders of Wildlife is one that needs to be high on your list.

Wonders of Wildlife also has Wildlife Galleries with immersive 4-D dioramas that transport you around the world—from the African savannah to the Arctic Circle—and even place you amongst a colony of live penguins.

500 W. Sunshine St., Springfield
888-222-6060, wondersofwildlife.org

OTHER MISSOURI AQUARIUMS

Aquarium at the Boardwalk
2700 W. 76 Country Blvd., Branson
aquariumattheboardwalk.com

Sea Life Aquarium
2475 Grand Blvd., Kansas City
visitsealife.com/kansas-city

St. Louis Aquarium at Union Station
201 S. 18th St., St. Louis
stlouisaquarium.com

EXPLORE
THE CITY MUSEUM

It's safe to say there is no other museum in the country quite like the City Museum. It's basically a museum in the former industrial section of St. Louis, along Washington Avenue, where many of the interactive exhibits are former architectural or industrial artifacts. The museum routinely wins international awards for its creativity and the way it engages visitors. Heck, it even has a Ferris Wheel on the roof! Formerly the home of the International Shoe Company, the massive facility has been remade into such a cool space that we sometimes describe it as the all-ages playground that Willy Wonka would've built. There is a 10-story slide, numerous caves, MonstroCity (the outdoor climbing gymasium/human Habitrail), and what they call the World's Largest Jungle Gym, for starters. A resident circus performs daily, and there is an artistic homage to the corn dog. This truly is a gem for the entire family that has to be experienced to be believed.

750 N. 16th St., St. Louis
314-231-2489, citymuseum.org

LAISSEZ LES BONS TEMPS ROULER
AT MARDI GRAS IN SOULARD

The second-largest Mardi Gras celebration in the United States takes place each year in the neighborhood south of downtown St. Louis, called Soulard. There are several events leading up to the festivities, like the Pet Parade and the Mayor's Mardi Gras Ball. Things kick into high gear with the Grand Parade, which packs tens of thousands of partygoers into the Soulard neighborhood streets to watch the parade and catch the beads from passing floats. The Krewes go from Busch Stadium to the Anheuser-Busch Brewery.

stlmardigras.org

TIP
If you really want to do the event like a rock star, purchase tickets to the Mayor's Ball and get decked out in your best themed outfit (depending on that year's theme.) It truly is one of the best parties of the year to see and be seen. Then, do the parade in style by getting tickets to one of the heated VIP tents along the parade route, like the Bud Light Party Tent. Typically, there are top-notch performers, along with plenty of food and drink . . . and heated bathrooms!

GET A TASTE OF GERMANY
DURING OKTOBERFEST IN HERMANN

Missouri's wine industry dates back nearly as long as Missouri has been a state. Much of that history was made by German immigrants who settled in the rolling hills along the Missouri River in the area now called Missouri's Rhineland. That culture and heritage are put on display each October in Hermann with a magnificent Oktoberfest that packs thousands of people into the small town resembling a German village that is nestled along the river.

Hermann is home to several wineries and breweries that are busy year-round, but they put on an extra-special show for the four weekends of October, when the leaves around town are turning beautiful shades of orange. If you don't feel like driving, several trolleys take visitors all over town to see the numerous shops and historical sites. If you feel like learning more about how Hermann came to be, you can spend an hour or two at the Historic Hermann Museum at the old German School or the Gasconade County Historical Society Archives.

150 Market St., Hermann
800-932-8687, visithermann.com

TIP

If you want to make a weekend trip of it, Hermann boasts dozens of bed and breakfasts, so you can enjoy all the winery tastings you want and won't have to worry about getting home. The only thing better than spending a Saturday at Oktoberfest in Hermann, is spending a Saturday and Sunday at Oktoberfest!

CROWN CENTER (page 67)
Photo courtesy of David Arborgast

FIRST STATE CAPITAL IN ST. CHARLES (page 99)

DOWNTOWN COLUMBIA (page 161)

DOGWOOD CANYON NATURE PARK (page 57)
Photo courtesy of Dogwood Canyon

TED DREWES (page 17)

ST. LOUIS AQUARIUM AT UNION STATION (page 110
Photo courtesy of St. Louis Aquarium at Union Station

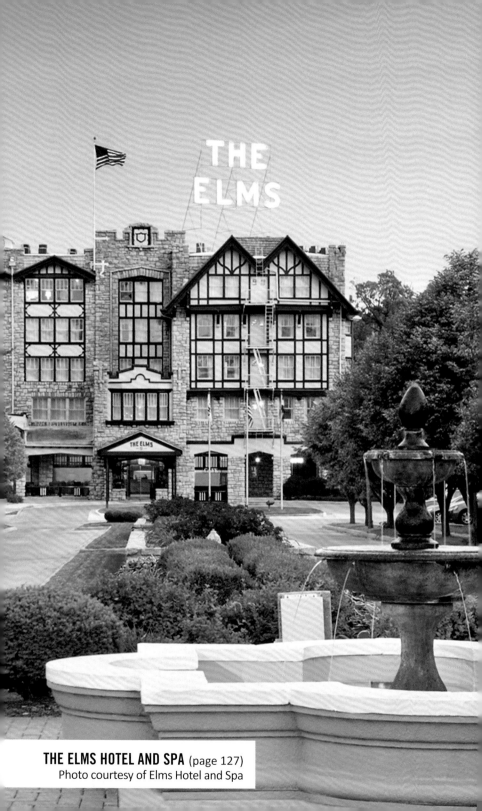

THE ELMS HOTEL AND SPA (page 127)
Photo courtesy of Elms Hotel and Spa

ANHEUSER-BUSCH (page 10)
Photo courtesy of David Lancaster

KANSAS CITY SKYLINE

ROUTE 66 FESTIVAL (page 120)

ARROW ROCK (page 112)

HANNIBAL (page 114)

SAINTE GENEVIEVE (page 156)

DRIVE SMART
ALONG THE "GENIUS HIGHWAY"

From the Mark Twain–inspired escapades of Huck, Tom, Becky, and Jim in Hannibal through the town of Marceline that was Walt Disney's childhood home and inspiration for the Main Street of his theme parks, US Highway 36 in north Missouri provides 195 miles of seriously good local lore. With longstanding status as a major east-west route—back to wagon trail days—today the road's been branded "the Way of American Genius," thanks to the important people and cultural contributions that originated there. Other significant stops include Chillicothe (original home of sliced bread, the literal best thing!) and St. Joseph, where the innovation of the Pony Express and its dogged riders take the spotlight. There are great, small museums and interesting sites at each stop—maybe you'll unleash your own Next Big Thing along the way!

Missouri Hwy. 36 Heritage Alliance
911 Frederick Ave., St. Joseph
816-233-6688, americangeniushighway.com

TIP
Almost exactly at the midpoint of U.S. 36 between Hannibal and St. Joseph, the Locust Creek Covered Bridge State Park houses the longest remaining covered bridge in the state (it's 151 feet across).

98

VISIT
MISSOURI'S FIRST STATE CAPITAL AND HISTORIC MAIN STREET IN ST. CHARLES

There are a few places in the Show-Me State where it feels like you're stepping back into a history book, yet everything still feels so fresh and new. St. Charles was the temporary capital of Missouri while the official seat of government was being established in Jefferson City, but a lot of history was made along those brick-paved streets. When you stop and read all the plaques, it really is hard to believe all that happened there, and that those homes and businesses are still in such amazing shape.

There are dozens of stores and cafes lining Main Street that should be explored. Many of the restaurants have outdoor dining, so Main Street is the perfect spot to watch the river go by, or watch the scores of people in the place that *Southern Living* magazine has dubbed "the Williamsburg of the West." If you have a bicycle, bring it along. The Katy Trail has plenty of access points along downtown St. Charles with places to park your bike, so you can grab a cup of coffee or a snack during your adventure.

If you visit during Christmastime, expect a special treat. Most of the stores are done up in Victorian-era decorations for the Christmas Traditions event, as the entire historic district becomes a magical wonderland.

200 S. Main St., St. Charles, 636-940-3322, mostateparks.com/park/ first-missouri-state-capitol-state-historic-site I discoverstcharles.com

STEP BACK INTO BASEBALL HISTORY
AT THE NEGRO LEAGUES BASEBALL MUSEUM

The history of the Negro Leagues comes to life in Kansas City's historic 18th and Vine Jazz District. If you are a fan of baseball, this multimedia museum is essential to understand the whole history of baseball in America. This museum brings to life the struggles that Black players faced, playing in their own league while striving to be treated as equals. This museum also celebrates the triumphs of these amazing players in what has been referred to as "the forgotten chapter" of baseball history. Even if you don't follow baseball, you will most certainly learn something about the era between the 1920s and 1960s to help understand our country's racial struggles better.

There are thousands of images, videos, and artifacts to help bring the stories to life. The Coors Field of Legends features statues of the legends of the Negro Leagues, while a locker area showcases the players who've been inducted into the Hall of Fame. You even will learn why Kansas City was so important to the origination of the Negro Leagues, and why it's so important for this museum to be based right here in Missouri!

1616 E. 18th St., Kansas City
888-221-6526, nlbm.com

FIND THE LUCK OF THE IRISH
ON BOTH SIDES OF THE STATE

One of the biggest St. Patrick's Day parades in the entire country takes place every year in the midtown area of Kansas City. How big is this parade? How about three hours long, with dozens of elaborate floats, marching bands, and green as far as the eye can see? This parade takes place on March 17 every year at Broadway and Linwood streets and heads south toward Westport. With all the cool bars and restaurants lining the parade route, it's a great way to spend the afternoon and evening, since many of your "new best friends" will be hanging out long after the parade is over.

For a bit o'the green that's just a bit different, head over to St. Louis. The Ancient Order of Hibernians St. Patrick's Day Parade in Dogtown is held on St. Patrick's Day every year, not on the weekend near the holiday. So, if you want to attend it, you might need to take the day off work (which we totally approve of). It's held in the small St. Louis neighborhood of Dogtown, near Forest Park. The majority of the parade runs on Tamm Avenue and passes several local establishments, which is handy for the hours after the conclusion of the parade. The event not only showcases the large Irish Catholic community in St. Louis, but also corresponds with the coming of spring, so the locals are ready to get out and mingle. This truly is one event that showcases the "best of the best" that the area has to offer.

kcirishparade.com | stlhibernians.com

SEE HOW THE WORLD WAS SAVED
AT THE NATIONAL WWI MUSEUM AND MEMORIAL

One of the most stunning monuments in Missouri stands just south of downtown Kansas City and honors the men and women who fought for our country in World War I. The National WWI Museum and Memorial was built just a few years after the conclusion of the war, based in large part on the strong support of the people from the Kansas City area who raised the money and spearheaded the effort. And this memorial goes above and beyond to show how the world rallied together to save humanity. It is home to one of the largest WWI collections in the world— more than 330,000 items strong. It's the only museum in the nation dedicated to sharing the stories of the Great War, through the eyes of those who lived it.

2 Memorial Dr., Kansas City
816-888-8100, theworldwar.org

TIP
Check out the exact replica of the Vietnam Veterans
Memorial in Perryville.
Missouri's National Veterans Memorial
1172 Veterans Memorial Pkwy., Perryville
573-547-2035, mnvmfund.org

DISCOVER
WHERE THE WILD WEST BEGAN

Much of what we think of as the "Wild West" traces its origins to St. Joseph. When you think of shootouts on horseback, cattle drives, the Pony Express, and the open frontier—pretty much all of that began along Missouri's western border. Start with the Patee House Museum, which was the headquarters for the Pony Express, in addition to being a luxury hotel. It now is home to the Pony Express Historical Association. A few blocks away is Pony Express National Museum, which tells more of the story of how mail was transported via horseback more than 2,000 miles to California. Next, check out the Jesse James Home, where the legendary outlaw was killed by fellow gang member Bob Ford. The Glore Psychiatric Museum is another stop that won't soon be forgotten. Seeing how doctors treated mentally ill patients in the days before modern medicine certainly will make you thankful you are alive today. And if you are a fan of magnificent homes, make time to drive Millionaire's Row on the Hall Street Historic District. At one time, St. Joseph had the highest per-capita income of any city in America, so yes, it's pretty impressive!

Patee House Museum
1202 Penn St., St. Joseph
816-232-8206
ponyexpressjessejames.com

Hall Street Historic District
Hall Street, Between 6th and 9th
Streets, St. Joseph

Glore Psychiatric Museum
3406 Frederick Ave., St. Joseph
stjosephmuseum.org/glore-psychiatric-museum

RELIVE HISTORY
AT THE CHURCHILL MUSEUM

One of the greatest leaders in world history made his mark on Missouri, and the world, during a speech called "The Sinews of Peace" at Westminster College in Fulton in 1946. Although most won't remember the title of Winston Churchill's speech, they will remember the phrase from the speech that changed the course of history . . . an "iron curtain has descended across the continent." After those words were uttered, the cold war was in full effect. America's National Churchill Museum, on the campus of Westminster College, still stands to tell the story of Churchill, along with artifacts from around the world that show his impact. World-renowned speakers still come to Fulton to take the dais, hoping to use his example to make the world a better place, as well.

501 Westminster Ave., Fulton
573-592-5369, nationalchurchillmuseum.org

VISIT
MISSOURI'S MOST FAMOUS LANDMARK

It's hard to believe that you have to encourage people to visit such an iconic place as Gateway Arch National Park, but still there are a significant number of people from the state who haven't experienced the tram ride that takes you to the top of America's tallest monument, 630 feet in the sky. The Gateway Arch is one of the most recognizable landmarks on the planet, and it sits right here as Missouri's symbol of westward expansion. Thanks to a nearly $400-million refurbishment of the 91-acre National Park site, which includes the historic Old Courthouse, everything looks fresh. From the monument's museum and visitor center, to the walkway connecting downtown St. Louis to the Arch, to the refreshed park grounds, it all feels new again. Particularly welcome is an enhanced focus in the exhibits on enlarging the perspectives to include those of native and enslaved people, whose own histories often have been erased in past celebrations of the monument. If you have never been, or even if you've been a dozen times, it might be time to check out the Gateway to the West's icon once again.

11 N. 4th St., St. Louis
877-982-1410, gatewayarch.com

TOUR
THE STATE CAPITOL...
WITH A GUIDE

There are some tours that you want to do by yourself and others that are done best with guidance. When it comes to the tour of the Missouri State Capitol, the latter certainly is better. Our magnificent seat of government stands on the banks of the Missouri River, where it is an imposing presence when you first see it. The bronze statue of Ceres stands on top of the domed roof more than 250 feet above ground level, which already is one of the highest points of Jefferson City. The giant columns flank the grand staircase, symbolizing the seat of power for a state that was born during a tipping point in American history. And if you want to hear more of that history come alive, it's worth your time to hear the stories from the knowledgeable experts inside.

Many of us have been inside the capitol for one reason or another over the years. But you obtain a new appreciation for the building and its history with the daily tours. You learn how the building was constructed, the stories of the artwork on the walls, the backgrounds of the famous Missourians who are immortalized in the halls, and stories of what really happens inside the chambers. It's a tour that leaves a lasting impression and provides a history lesson that is not soon forgotten.

201 W. Capitol Ave., Jefferson City
573-751-2854, mostateparks.com/page/55186/missouri-state-capitol

TIP

Do not miss the House Lounge (and its nifty automatic doors), where enormous murals commissioned from artist Thomas Hart Benton stretch across the walls, telling the stories of many different kinds of Missourians through different historical eras. Benton doesn't shy away from the good, the bad, or the ugly . . . although he renders it all beautifully.

CHECK OUT
THE REAL TRUMAN SHOW

At this point in American history, Missouri still has only one US President as a native son. That makes it a necessity to put the Truman Presidential Library and Home on your list, because it literally is a one-of-a-kind spot in our state. You'll develop a greater understanding about Truman during one afternoon in Independence than you could ever learn from a history book. It will give you a new perspective on the monumental decisions this Missourian had to make during his time in office, and how he literally changed the world. Presidential libraries are designed to be a celebration of the accomplishments of these great Americans, and this one certainly is no exception. It's a great time to visit, since the facility underwent a massive renovation in 2020.

500 W. US Hwy. 24, Independence
816-268-8200, trumanlibrary.gov

TIP
If you want the full Truman experience, you also can visit the longtime home of President Truman at 219 N. Delaware St. in Independence. This was where Harry and his wife, Bess Wallace, lived from the time they were married until his death in 1972. The home actually was built by Bess' grandfather. The former First Lady lived there until she died in 1982, when it was bequeathed to the National Park Service.

SEE THE INSPIRATION
FOR *LITTLE HOUSE ON THE PRAIRIE*

Millions of Americans grew up reading Laura Ingalls Wilder's Little House on the Prairie books and fell in love with her stories about pioneer life. Millions more were exposed to the lifestyle with the TV series of the same name. That's why tens of thousands of people still flock to Rocky Ridge Farm every year to see the inspiration for her writings.

Typically, in early October, the city of Mansfield hosts Wilder Day. It's their annual celebration of all things celebrating Laura Ingalls Wilder and her Little House books. This is one of the best times to tour the farm and the quaint small town. There is plenty of fiddle music to be heard, along with crafts and other festivities taking place in both locations. Plus, the weather typically has cooled off and it's perfect for walking, so you can fully embrace Wilder's spirit of the wide-open spaces described in her books.

3060 State Hwy. A, Mansfield
417-924-3626, lauraingallswilderhome.com

SEE HISTORY
IN A NEW LIGHT
AT ST. LOUIS UNION STATION

St. Louis Union Station has been a part of the city's history since 1894, but recent changes have given the old rail station a facelift. Sure, the National Historic Landmark train station has undergone numerous changes over the years—even a shopping mall in the 1980s—but the latest changes offer a taste of history, while bringing the classic station into the present.

Outside, in the train shed, the St. Louis Wheel now stands. The 42-gondola observation wheel takes you 200 feet in the air with amazing views of the city in all directions. There also are a pair of restaurants, including the Soda Fountain, which serves some of the most amazing ice cream Freak Shakes you will find anywhere. There also is a nightly Fire and Light show on the lake when the sun goes down.

Inside the train station, you'll find the St. Louis Aquarium at Union Station, which opened on December 25, 2019. The 120,000 square feet of water exhibits feature 257 species of fresh- and saltwater animals, including sharks, otters, and pretty much everything else under the sea, for a total of 13,000 animals.

The Grand Lobby remains much the same as it looked in the early 1900s, only better. A magnificent entry to a marvelous structure still welcomes visitors. But in the evenings, the Grand Hall Experience 3D Light Show, set to music, is projected onto the barrel-vaulted ceiling for a one-of-a-kind show. The hotel has been redone, with some of the rooms now encompassing the old clock tower and named for the former train companies that called St. Louis home, if you want the ultimate St. Louis experience.

1820 Market St., St. Louis
314- 621-5262, stlouisunionstation.com

TIP

Join the generations of secret-sharers who've sent sweet nothings (or juicy somethings!) through the air via the acoustic trick known as the Whispering Arch. Position yourselves at opposite ends of the arched doorway that faces Market Street, and turn to face the wall. Whatever you whisper will travel over the archway and to your companion on the other side.

WALK MISSOURI'S
EARLY HISTORY

There are some small towns in Missouri that can be called quintessential Missouri towns—they just emanate Missouri history. Arrow Rock is one of them. In fact, the entire town is listed as a part of the National Historic Landmark Arrow Rock Historic District and the Lewis and Clark and Santa Fe National Historic Trail. Even though the small village has dwindled in population over the course of history, if you consider yourself a Missouri history buff, visiting Arrow Rock is a critical piece of a full understanding of the story of our state.

This village of 56 residents (according to the most recent census) routinely attracts about 100,000 visitors annually. They come to see the homes and museums of famous early residents like artist George Caleb Bingham and Dr. John Sappington, the quinine doctor. The Lyceum Theater and J. Huston Tavern, the oldest continually operating restaurant west of the Mississippi, also are favorites for locals and tourists alike. As you might expect, if you want to stay the night, it's best to book early. With such a disparity between residents and visitors, many of the better B&Bs and the adjacent state park campground book weeks in advance.

Arrow Rock State Historic Site
39521 Visitor Center Dr., Arrow Rock
660-837-3330, mostateparks.com/park/arrow-rock-state-historic-site

J. Huston Tavern
305 Main St., Arrow Rock
660-837-3200

EXPLORE
THE MISSOURI BOTANICAL GARDEN

There are a plethora of reasons to visit the Missouri Botanical Garden. The famous garden was founded way back in 1859 and now claims the distinction of being the country's oldest botanical garden in continuous operation.

Most people immediately recognize the dome-shaped Climatron, which houses a tropical rainforest, when you drive past the garden on Interstate 44, just west of St. Louis. But that is just a small portion of what the site has to offer. There are the Japanese Garden, the George Washington Carver Garden, and nearly 80 acres of some of the most beautifully manicured grounds you will find anywhere. And if you are an architectural history buff, you will certainly enjoy learning about Tower Grove House, which was built for wealthy St. Louisan Henry Shaw, the founder of the garden.

All of those are fine reasons to visit. But special events and concerts throughout the year make the garden just a little more special. From the orchid shows to the Japanese Festival, and from the Whitaker Music Festival to the Garden Glow during the holidays, there is never a wrong time to visit the garden.

4344 Shaw Blvd., St. Louis
314-577-5100, missouribotanicalgarden.org

VISIT
MARK TWAIN'S BOYHOOD HOME

There are a handful of Missouri attractions that are famous primarily for events that happened there, or for the famous people who called that place their home. Hannibal is one of those places. Thousands of people from around the world still flock to the Mississippi River town annually to see the inspiration for one of America's most beloved authors, Samuel Clemens— better known as Mark Twain.

There are several ways to experience Mark Twain's childhood home. You can do the self-guided version, or take part in any one of several guided tours around the town. But no matter what you choose, there are several stops along the way that must be included for you to get a good understanding of the Hannibal that influenced a young Clemens.

TIP

Hannibal is a beautiful river city, so make time to walk the city streets and grab a bite to eat or a cup of coffee at one of the downtown establishments. If you happen to make the trip to Hannibal during the summer, there is a free concert series on Thursday nights called Music Under the Stars on historic Hill Street. There also is a western-themed Twain on Main festival on Memorial Day weekend, which is dedicated to celebrating the life and works of Mark Twain.

• •

The Mark Twain Boyhood Home and Museum is an obvious starting place. This gives you the opportunity to see where he spent his formative years. It includes his home and gardens, but also includes admission to the real home where Huck Finn (Tom Blankenship) lived, along with the Becky Thatcher (Laura Hawkins) House, and other important places from his life and books. There also are impersonators in town who give a better idea of his life story. A newer addition is **Jim's Journey: The Huck Finn Freedom Center**, which takes a different tack in exploring how Twain's writing treated the lives of his Black characters.

Mark Twain Boyhood Home & Museum
120 N. Main St., Hannibal
573-221-9010, marktwainmuseum.org

Jim's Journey: The Huck Finn Freedom Center
509 N. 3rd St., Hannibal
217-617-1507, jimsjourney.org

• •

GET INSPIRED DIVINELY
AT THE CATHEDRAL BASILICA

For some people, it may seem strange to walk into a place of worship as a tourist, but that is exactly what parishioners expect at the Cathedral Basilica in the Central West End neighborhood of St. Louis. And who wouldn't? When you attend one of the most beautiful churches in the entire world, welcoming pilgrims comes with the territory.

The Mother Church of the Archdiocese of St. Louis was designated as a Cathedral Basilica by Pope Saint John Paul II in 1997. The Cathedral celebrated its 100th anniversary in 2014, and it keeps getting more magnificent as each generation adds something new. In fact, it took nearly 80 years for all of the mosaic tiles to be put in place in place on the walls and ceiling.

Thousands of people walk into the church annually to look around and absorb the majesty of the superstructure. Some will stop to pray, others will just take it all in. There is nothing wrong with walking around to see the many areas of worship inside the cathedral. There also is a museum in the basement where you can pay for admission to get the entire backstory on the history of the Basilica and what it took to make the building a reality. Once you have been inside the Cathedral Basilica, it's really hard for most anything else, outside of Rome, to compare.

4431 Lindell Blvd., St. Louis
cathedralstl.org

TIP

You can check off a "biggest and best" from your life list here, as the Cathedral Basilica is home to the biggest collection of mosaic art under one roof.

SPEND A DAY ...
OR TWO ...
IN FOREST PARK

It would be hard to fit everything there is to be done in Forest Park into one day and truly experience it all fully. After all, as locals like to tell you, Forest Park is one of the largest urban parks in the entire country—and bigger than New York's Central Park, thank you very much. So, with a little planning, you can pack it all in and learn quite a bit about the history of the amazing park along the way, which also was home to the 1904 World's Fair.

The best place to begin is the Dennis & Judith Jones Visitor and Education Center. That way, you can grab a map and read some of the history on the walls before you begin. Plus, it's a short jaunt to the Missouri History Museum. Spending the morning reading about the place you're visiting will help put into context many of the things you are about to see. Knowing how the Saint Louis Zoo began and how the Emerson Grand Basin was formed, with the Art Museum looking down from above, will give a greater appreciation for this amazing park. As the morning wraps up, lunch at the Boathouse at Forest Park is a must before venturing over to the Saint Louis Art Museum. If you have time during your visit in the summer, an afternoon in the museum is perfect, because that gives you just enough time to get ready for Shakespeare in the Park in the evening or a show at the Muny, which is America's oldest and largest outdoor musical theater.

The following day is set aside for the world-famous Saint Louis Zoo. There is no finer zoological park anywhere in the world than Saint Louis, where you can see 13,000 animals representing 555 species, including several endangered species. Follow that with a trip to the Saint Louis Science Center, where more than 700 interactive exhibits will challenge the curiosity of both young and old.

It's important also to point out that all of the attractions are FREE! Oh, wait, we forgot to mention one more free attraction: a brand-new 17-acre Nature Playscape in the park next to the Saint Louis Zoo. There are eight activity areas, including mounds, a spring, a meadow, a wetland, and more. A series of paths and boardwalks connect the distinct areas, creating opportunities for kids and families to climb, splash, build, and explore their way through the site. What other city can boast attractions of this scale that are supported entirely by individual and corporate philanthropy?

forestparkforever.org

GET YOUR KICKS
IN THE BIRTHPLACE OF ROUTE 66

Since US Route 66 officially got its name in the city of Springfield, it only seems fitting that you spend a little time on the Mother Road in the city that gave it birth. The Queen City of the Ozarks officially is recognized as the birthplace of Route 66, because it was at the old Colonial Hotel that a telegram was sent which proposed that the name of this new road from Chicago to Los Angeles be named US 66. And there is no better time to "get your kicks" on Route 66 than during the Birthplace of Route 66 Festival, which takes place in August around the historic downtown Springfield square. You also can go back in time with the recently opened History Museum on the Square downtown, that gives you an excellent perspective on how the road and the city developed around each other. The museum was recently named *USA Today*'s Best New Attraction in the United States for 2020, so it is well worth the trip.

Birthplace of Route 66 Festival
route66festivalsgf.com

History Museum on the Square
154 Park Central Sq., Springfield
417-831-1976, historymuseumonthesquare.org

TOUR
THE "BLOODIEST 47 ACRES IN AMERICA"

Although the Missouri State Penitentiary was NOT a place you wanted to visit for the first 168 years of its existence, the "old state pen" now is a pretty cool place to visit. The penitentiary opened in 1836 in downtown Jefferson City, along the banks of the Missouri River, and housed some of the most notorious inmates in America until it was decommissioned in 2004. It now offers a variety of tours, so you can see what life was like behind the walls and razor wire and why *Time Magazine* once named it "The bloodiest 47 acres in America."

The Missouri State Penitentiary is a rare prison that housed both male and female inmates. Some of the more infamous names include James Earl Ray, Charles "Pretty Boy" Floyd, and Charles "Sonny" Liston. Over the years, 40 inmates were put to death in the gas chamber on the grounds at the prison, leading many to believe the prison is haunted (the basis for one of the tours that is offered).

Although some people may consider it morbid, there is quite a history lesson to be learned at the Missouri State Penitentiary. You can take part in several tours, including a mystery tour, private tours, student tours, and, of course, the ghost and paranormal tours. The eight-hour, overnight, paranormal investigation tour even lets you spend the night!

115 Lafayette St., Jefferson City
866-998-6998, missouripentours.com

COMMUNE WITH THE FOREBEARS
AT BELLEFONTAINE AND CALVARY CEMETERIES

The folks in charge of grand, historic cemeteries these days know that a stereotype of sad or stodgy—or maybe even creepy—isn't going to get them anywhere. So they've done a lot of outreach to make their parklike acres a place anyone would want to visit, to see the resting places of some of the folks (famous, infamous, and everything in between) who put St. Louis on the map. Frequent tours and special events, including Beer Barons and Women of Note, reveal the sometimes-spectacular permanent residences of notables, from Adolphus Busch to Sara Teasdale. Other famous folks buried here include explorer William Clark and writer William S. Burroughs. Nestled next door to Bellefontaine is the Catholic counterpart, Calvary Cemetery; prominent people in repose here include city founder René Auguste Chouteau, Kate Chopin, Tennessee Williams, and Dred Scott. Let the history lessons begin.

Bellefontaine
4947 W. Florissant Ave., St. Louis
314-381-0750, bellefontainecemetery.org

Calvary
5239 W. Florissant Ave., St. Louis
314-792-7738, cemeteries.archstl.org/Locations/Calvary

TIP

Civil War buffs will find plenty of interest here. More generals who commanded troops (on both sides of the conflict) are buried in these two cemeteries than at Arlington National Cemetery and West Point combined.

REMEMBER THE CIVIL WAR
AT WILSON'S CREEK

A border state with passions high on all sides of the conflict, Missouri has a complicated history with regard to the Civil War. Slavery was legal, but secession never happened. Urban centers and rural outposts were in constant conflict, and the enmity tore apart neighbors and families. For our state, the first major action happened on August 10, 1861. The fighting took place at Wilson's Creek, where the state's former (Confederate-sympathetic) leadership had gone to muster support for a takeover. Federal forces followed and tried to vanquish them in a surprise attack, and a day-long battle raged. Casualties were heavy: more than 1,000 troops on each side died. The Southern forces eventually won the day, but at great cost; they also were unable to translate that battlefield victory into success in dislodging Missouri from the Union. This site details it all, with a self-guided, five-mile driving tour of significant stops. The freshly upgraded visitor center includes tons of exhibit space for the expansive collections of Wilson's Creek National Battlefield, as well as interactive and virtual displays.

6424 W. Farm Rd. 182, Republic
417-732-2662, nps.gov/wicr/index.htm

TIP

The state is full of places with a Civil War connection, but you can find a comprehensive overview at the Missouri Civil War Museum at Jefferson Barracks, an active military installation south of St. Louis; mcwm.org.

HITCH A RIDE
ACROSS THE STATE ON AMTRAK

There is just something magical about touring the countryside via train, and the trip between Missouri's two biggest cities is one that you shouldn't miss. The Missouri River Runner Amtrak route runs between St. Louis and Kansas City and operates several times per day. Along the way, you will go through scenic towns like Washington, Hermann, Jefferson City, Sedalia, Warrensburg, Lee's Summit, and Independence. The one drawback? Often, the train gets delayed due to other trains using the tracks across the state, but if you plan on the trip taking the better part of the day, and know you are there to take in the sights, you can just sit back and enjoy. It's best to start on one side of the state, plan to spend the night with a good dinner on the other side, and ride back the following morning. After all, it's about experiencing Missouri in unique ways and checking those experiences off your bucket list!

amtrak.com/missouri-river-runner-train

INDULGE
AT THE ELMS HOTEL AND SPA AND EXCELSIOR SPRINGS HALL OF WATERS

There was a period of time, starting in the late 1800s, when health-conscious Americans flocked to Excelsior Springs to sample the water that locals said would cure all sorts of ailments. The water that flowed from 10 mineral springs in the area, about 30 miles northeast of Kansas City, became famous as the area was dubbed "America's Haven of Health." Because of that fame, The Elms Hotel was built so the rich and famous (even presidential) guests, along with everyday people, could pamper and renew themselves in the mineral-rich waters. Although the springs no longer are the draw they used to be, there are numerous historic buildings around town, like the Hall of Waters Visitors Center—an incredibly ornate building that takes you back in time and tells the story in a way you have to experience. The Elms Hotel still is a top-notch hotel and spa that combines historical charm with present-day indulgences.

Excelsior Springs
201 E. Broadway Ave., Excelsior Springs
816-637-2811, visitexcelsior.com

The Elms Hotel and Spa
401 Regent St., Excelsior Springs
816-630-5500, elmshotelandspa.com

VISIT
THE AMISH COMMUNITY
IN JAMESPORT

Sometimes the best road trips are to the out-of-the-way places where you can just slow down for the day. That certainly is true of a trip to Jamesport, which is about an hour east of St. Joseph. Jamesport is a snapshot of how Missouri used to be, about 50 years ago, thanks in large part to the large Amish community that calls this area home. This day trip is a chance to see how a truly unique community thrives in the 2020s, and an opportunity to purchase fresh and handmade items that you know, without a doubt, are made right here in Missouri. If you want to see the community at its finest, plan to attend the Heritage Days in September, although there are festivals and other events throughout the year where families display their goods and services.

jamesport-mo.com

> **TIP**
> Please respect the Amish prohibition against having their photographs made, and keep your cameras stowed.

SET OUT
ON THE LEWIS AND CLARK EXPEDITION

Given Missouri's status as the Gateway to the West, residents here have been saying, "Farewell, and hope to see you soon" to folks for a long time—perhaps none more famous than Meriwether Lewis, William Clark, and their small band of intrepid explorers. Charged by President Thomas Jefferson with figuring out what lay within the western scope of the country's Louisiana Purchase, they set out from a spot north of St. Charles in 1804. The Lewis & Clark Boat House and Museum features replica keelboats from the mission, along with indoor exhibits on the flora and fauna the group encountered on the journey. It's a small facility, but the second-floor exhibit space offers a sweeping view of the Missouri River through its large windows. Make sure the kids get a scavenger hunt sheet and pencil from the desk on their way in!

1050 S. Riverside Dr., St. Charles
636-947-3199, lewisandclarkcenter.org

TIP
Can't get enough L&C? Wait till you're hungry for lunch or dinner and head down the cobblestones to Lewis & Clark's American Restaurant.

217 S. Main St., St. Charles
636-947-3334

ROUGH IT
WITH DANIEL BOONE

One of the most famous of all American frontiersmen, Daniel Boone was born in Pennsylvania. He lived in North Carolina, Florida, Virginia, and, of course, Kentucky . . . and ended up in Defiance, Missouri. In his prime, Boone cleared the 200-mile Wilderness Road through the Appalachian Mountains with his team, founded forts (and then fought the native people who tried to eject them from their hunting grounds), and became a global celebrity when a hagiographic book featured tales of his exploits. When he arrived in Missouri in the 1790s, it was to join his son, Nathan, and he lived from age 65 until his death in 1820 on the property. Today, the Historic Daniel Boone Home site encompasses a replica frontier village, complete with a dozen period buildings, from a schoolhouse to a grist mill.

1868 State Hwy. F, Defiance
636-798-2005, sccmo.org/1701/the-historic-daniel-boone-home

TIP

When you're ready to return to the present, you're also in beautiful wine country. We recommend repairing to the extensive outdoor patio at Chandler Hill Winery.

596 Defiance Rd., Defiance
636-798-2675, chandlerhillvineyards.com

81

CELEBRATE MISSOURI
AT THE STATE FAIR

There is just something about the Missouri State Fair that gathers everything that makes our state great, together in one place. The state fair has convened in Sedalia since 1901, and continues to be one of the biggest and best state celebrations in the entire country. From the livestock competitions to possibly meeting your elected leaders at the Governor's Ham Breakfast, it seems everyone in a position of state leadership somehow ends up at the fair. The fair committee always lands some of the best touring entertainers every year and, of course, the midway rides are a perennial favorite. One thing certainly you will find: everyone lets down their guard and wants to talk, from the powerful to the general public. It truly is the nicest collection of people you will find in one place.

2503 W. 16th St., Sedalia
800-422-3247, mostatefair.com

EXPERIENCE
THE MAPLE LEAF FESTIVAL
IN CARTHAGE

The Maple Leaf Festival brings more than 80,000 people to Carthage every year to celebrate autumn. The vibrant leaves on the Historic Square the third Saturday of October are the backdrop for the biggest parade in all of southwest Missouri each year. The festival dates to 1966 as a marching band festival, but has transitioned over the years to include a car and tractor show, along with food vendors, live entertainment, plenty of arts and crafts, and much more. The town was an important part of Missouri's Civil War history, so why not block off the entire weekend, enjoy the fun, and see the sights at the same time?

carthagemapleleaf.com/maple-leaf

TIP
While in Carthage, also make time to check out the Precious Moments Chapel and Gardens. This is so much more than just the tiny figurines. This is a place of awe.

4321 S. Chapel Rd., Carthage
800-543-7975, preciousmomentschapel.org

MARVEL
AT THE BRILLIANCE
OF GEORGE WASHINGTON CARVER

From the humblest of beginnings—born into an enslaved family on a Missouri farm in the mid-1800s—sprang a mind so nimble and adaptive that, even today, we still are amazed by the accomplishments of George Washington Carver. A scientist most renowned for his work with the peanut plant, he also was a brilliant teacher and mentor, an inventor, a writer, and much more. He was the first African American to have a national monument dedicated in his honor. The site, near Diamond, retains a house built by the couple who raised him as their own, Moses and Susan Carver, who are buried on the property. A visitor center showcases George's scientific achievements and legacy.

5646 Carver Rd., Diamond
417-325-4151, nps.gov/gwca/index.htm

TIP
For hands-on experimentation,
check out the schedule of classes and
activities offered in the Carver Science
Classroom, modeled on one of Carver's labs
at the Tuskegee Institute in Alabama.

DRIVE
THROUGH WILD ANIMAL SAFARI

Across the state are several world-class zoos, which are listed throughout this book. But there is one zoological park that has the unique distinction of being called one of the best drive-through animal parks in the country. That's Wild Animal Safari in Strafford. It has been known for years as "Exotic Animal Paradise" along Interstate 44 in southwest Missouri, and it's such a unique way to experience wild animals in their own habitat. You either can drive through in your own vehicle, or you can do the tour inside the park's tour bus so you can hear the full story from the expert tour guides. After you ride through the park, there is an additional area where you can do a "walk-about" to see more wild animals in a more typical zoo setting.

124 Jungle Dr., Strafford
417-859-5300, animalsafari.com/MO

OTHER MISSOURI ZOOS

Swope Park Zoo
6800 Zoo Dr., Kansas City
816-595-1234, kansascityzoo.org

Springfield Zoo
1401 W. Norton Rd., Springfield
417-833-1570, dickersonparkzoo.org

Grant's Farm
10501 Gravois Rd., St. Louis
314-577-2626, grantsfarm.com

Saint Louis Zoo
1 Government Dr., St. Louis
314-781-0900, stlzoo.org

UNCOVER NATIVE HISTORY
AT VAN METER STATE PARK

Missouri's been here for a lot longer than it's been "Missouri," and several significant spots help illuminate the evidence of the first peoples who walked these lands. A comprehensive overview of nine major tribes (including the Otoe-Missouria Indians) who occupied what became Missouri starts at Missouri's American Indian Cultural Center at Van Meter State Park. Large-scale maps and portraits set the stage for artifact displays, many of which were unearthed at a nearby settlement. The history crosses into European arrival with the inclusion of William Clark (yes, the explorer), who served as Superintendent of Indian Affairs in the early 1800s.

MORE SITES OF NATIVE HERITAGE

To see a remaining (if far off the beaten path) example of the Mississippian mound builder culture typified by the people who preceded Europeans here, make your way to Towosahgy State Historic Site. Remnants of ceremonial mounds and a civic plaza, dating from a period from the years 400-1400, are visible, along with several explanatory markers. Another reminder of the Mississippian past surfaces at Washington State Park, home to a large collection of remarkably well preserved petroglyphs. Finally, a less celebratory (but no less important) commemoration of the fate of the native people of the region is documented in exhibits and interpretive programming at Trail of Tears State Park: thousands of Cherokee people on a forced march from their home to reservations in Oklahoma passed this way, and many died in the harsh winters they spent here.

Van Meter State Park
32146 N. State Rte. 122, Miami
660-886-7537, mostateparks.com/park/
annie-and-abel-van-meter-state-park

Towosahgy State Historic Site
County Rd. 502, East Prairie
573-748-5340, mostateparks.com/park/
towosahgy-state-historic-site

Washington State Park
13041 State Rte. 104, De Soto
636-586-5768, mostateparks.com/park/washington-state-park

Trail of Tears State Park
429 Moccasin Springs, Jackson
573-290-5268, mostateparks.com/park/trail-tears-state-park

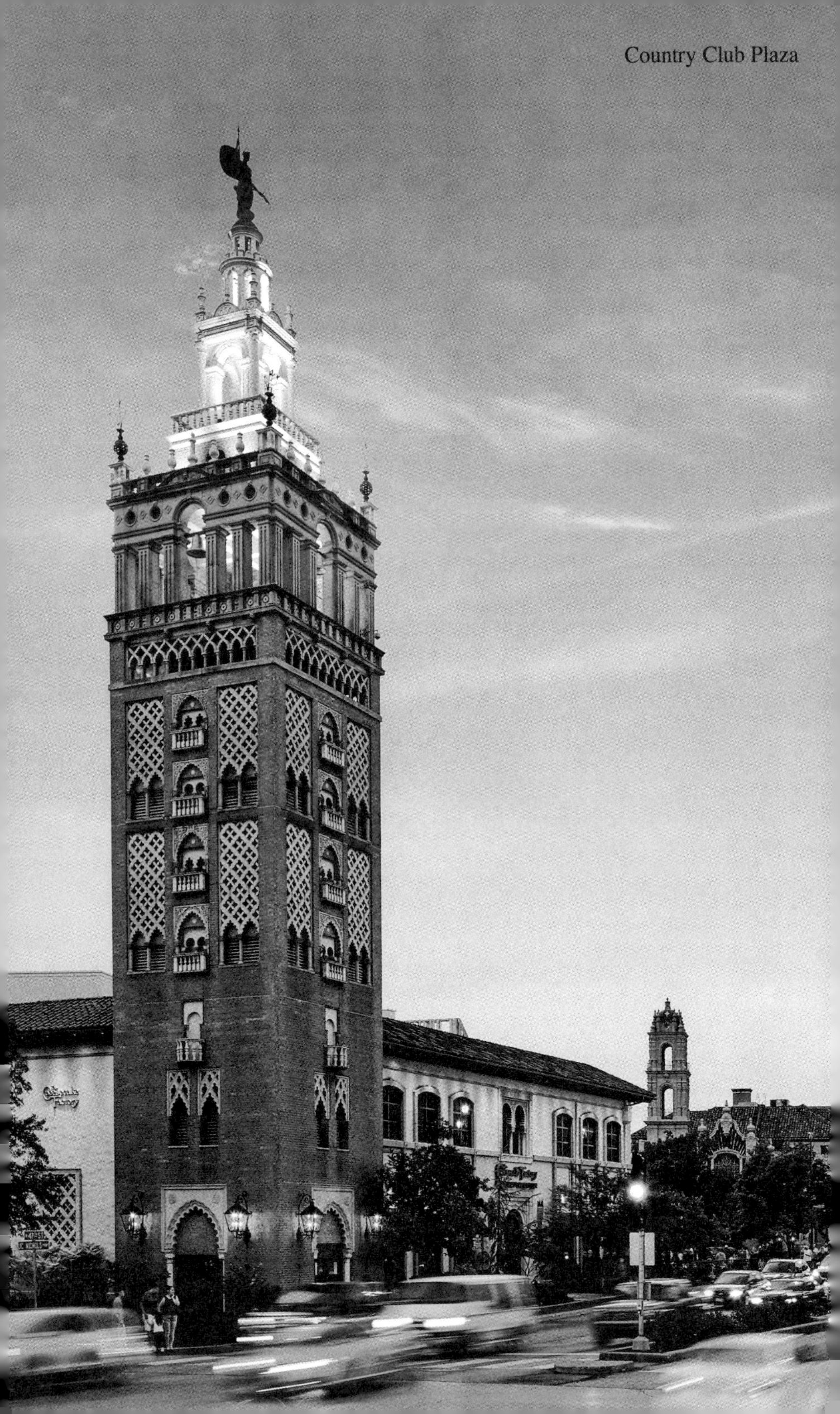

Country Club Plaza

SHOPPING AND FASHION

MARVEL AT
WHAT HANDS CAN MAKE
AT MADISON FLITCH

Craftsman and founder John Pryor had a vision when he started Madison Flitch handmade furniture a few years back: "tree to table" fine furnishings and home goods sourced from urban trees in the metro Kansas City area, cut/planed/dried under his oversight, and transformed into their next lives as tables, benches, trays, and accent pieces. Oh, and it's all done by hand, no screws/ bolts required. It's not the easiest or cheapest way to make furniture, but it's been the perfect landing for a polymath whose past encompasses jobs in corporate technology and degrees in history and theology. The thoroughly modern pieces that emerge from the studio have global appeal, with all-Missouri heart.

501 E. 16th St., Kansas City
madisonflitch.com

TIP

Don't miss the side project, Madison Stitch, started in 2020 as a way for talented sewists (including many refugees from Myanmar and Afghanistan) to produce masks when the pandemic struck the city. The line recently unveiled handbags and totes created by those same women.

BUY MISSOURI
AT WILLOW SPRING MERCANTILE

We feel like you support local (look at the book you're holding . . .). So, make some time to browse the delightful offerings at this quaint shop in downtown Excelsior Springs—they claim the state's biggest selection of Missouri wines, craft beers, and distilled spirits. That distinction, plus their boutique of everything from local beeswax candles to handmade (and hilarious) tea towels, means you could cover a lot of your gift list in a single store. If you've managed to shop till you want to drop, you're covered. A small bistro serves lunch and occasional special-event dinners. Wine tastings and live music add the finishing touches.

249 E. Broadway, Excelsior Springs
816-630-7467, shopthemercantile.com

TIP
Always say "yes" to whatever dessert is coming out of the oven, be it peach pie with local peaches or lemon-poppyseed layer cake.

WEAR YOUR HEART ON YOUR TEE
AT CHARLIE HUSTLE

Charlie Hustle just wants to be loved. Kansas City's T-shirt-ier of choice blew up with its signature KC Heart design a few years ago, and founder Chase MacAnulty says all they want to be is your favorite: "Favorite T-shirt, favorite brand, favorite message." You may not think a shirt can change the world, but think back to the team, or the band, or the college, or the neighborhood that made you, that was everything to you, and boom: you've hit upon the nexus of vintage passion and modern ease these tees aim to project. Rock the Arrowhead Stadium design, rep your favorite BBQ, or keep it simple with the classic heart.

419 W. 47th St., Kansas City
816-541-4387, charliehustle.com

TIP

Don't worry, St. Louis, we've got you covered, too! The twin brothers (Jeff and Randy Vines) who own STL Style make iconic tees featuring everything from the Bevo Mill to "Highway Farty," and nearly every city neighborhood in between.

3159 Cherokee St., St. Louis
314-898-0001, stl-style.com

PLANT YOURSELF
AT BAKER CREEK HEIRLOOM SEED COMPANY

Fitting that here, near the prairie legend that Laura Ingalls Wilder built (see page 109 for more), this family-owned seed company dedicated to the old ways—and the heirloom vegetables—has sprouted up. Founders Jere and Emilee Gettle and their four children look the part, too. Their old-timey aesthetic sets the tone for the 19th-century way of life their ancestors on this land might've known.

The seeds here are open-pollinated, non-hybridized, and not the result of genetic engineering. Jere scours the globe for unusual, hardy plants to include in his annual Whole Seed Catalog, which is a thing of beauty, itself. Page after page of vegetables, from old stalwarts to exotic imports, will keep gardeners up late, plotting purchases for their next planting season.

2278 Baker Creek Rd., Mansfield
417-924-8887, rareseeds.com

TIP
Several annual festivals at the Baker Creek site draw huge crowds for natural food demos, old-time music, and much more.

CRACK THE CODE
AT PUZZLE WAREHOUSE

Let's be clear: 53,000 square feet holds a lot of puzzles. That's the combined footprint (retail shop and warehouse) of St. Louis's Puzzle Warehouse, which gives it a great degree of confidence in proclaiming itself the "Largest Jigsaw Puzzle Store in the USA." And from four-piece toddler diversions to a 40,320-piece puzzle they stock, you will be gobsmacked by the variety filling their shelves. Top brands like Ravensburger and MasterPieces are well-represented, but it's not just traditional jigsaw puzzles to entertain you. The store also sells party games, brain teasers, kids' toys, and even accessories like puzzle mats and fixatives. With as much time as we've all spent at home lately, isn't it time to restock your puzzle and game drawer?

655 Leffingwell Ave., St. Louis
314-856-4030, puzzlewarehouse.com

TIP
A little puzzling trivia for you: do you know which piece-count sells the best? If you said 1,000, you are correct!

MAKE AN IMPRESSION
AT HAMMERPRESS

If you have a friend who always has just the right card, or gives the perfect, just-so gifts, it might be time to pay her back with a little something from this letterpress print shop and stationer in the Crossroads District of Kansas City. Using metal or wood plates containing the type elements, and a vintage press, the shop's design side can turn out everything from quirky greeting cards to custom band posters or wedding invitations. The retail shop sells the printed products alongside a fabulously curated selection of desk accessories, stationery extras, candles, textiles, and writing implements.

1413 W. 11th St., Kansas City
816-421-1929, hammerpress.net

TIP
You can get hands-on at Hammerpress in one of their popular workshops; try making your own letterpress holiday cards.

SHOP POSH
AT COUNTRY CLUB PLAZA

When the Plaza, as it's often shorthanded, debuted in 1923, the new reality became quite clear: this was the first planned suburban shopping district in the country, and the first that understood the needs of customers arriving by automobile. Decades later, this 15-block area still draws shoppers and strollers, thanks in equal measure to its distinctive and elaborate Moorish architecture, the dozens of eye-catching fountains scattered throughout, and the high-end retail experiences that online shopping just can't deliver.

When the winter holidays roll around, Christmas lights and window displays transform the district during the Plaza Lights celebration. Carolers and horse-drawn carriage rides help set the stage for all the holiday cheer you can imagine.

47th and Broadway, Kansas City
816-753-0100, countryclubplaza.com

TIP
Musical acts, celebrity switch-flippers, and fireworks fill the schedule on Thanksgiving evening, the official kickoff to Plaza Lights each year.

SOAK UP THE SOUNDS
AT VINTAGE VINYL

You don't have to be a hard-core crate digger to get into the groove at Vintage Vinyl, the 40-year stalwart of independent record stores in St. Louis. Go in, start with something you already know, and before long the handmade signage, multiple listening booths, enthusiastic staff, and live-mixed soundtrack will lead you down the rabbit hole of musical discovery. The local artist section is, of course, especially strong, but this is where you'll find serious fans flipping through the hidden gems that collectors on the coasts can't lay their hands on. Outside the store, buskers and other street performers do their earnest best to convince passers-by they're the Next Big Thing. (A few actually have been!) And keep an eye on the marquee sign: it's a catalog of the earthly comings and goings of some of music's luminaries.

6610 Delmar Blvd., St. Louis
314-721-4096, vintagevinyl.com

TIP
Beyond the vinyl and CDs, the store stocks some of the coolest band tees, show posters, concert DVDs, and other pop-culture merch.

MORE GREAT RECORD STORES

Euclid Records
especially strong in jazz recordings
(fitting, since they have a sister store in New Orleans)
19 N. Gore, Webster Groves
314-961-8978, euclidrecords.com

Heavy Heads Records
tons of vinyl (and vintage and professional audio gear)
215 W. Olive, Springfield
417-228-0084, heavyheadsrecords.com

Rinehart's Music and Video
a bit of a mishmash, with records/CDs/cassettes/coins/video
games/collectibles/sheet music/player piano rolls (yes,
really). Worth a look, though, as it claims to be the
oldest record store in the country, dating to 1897!
114 S. Franklin St., Kirksville
facebook.com/Rinehartsmusicandvideo

GotWhatULike Records
Owner Mark Harper started re-collecting vinyl and audio
equipment (that he'd lost in his teens), until the stacks
overtook a storage shed, and then migrated to a proper store
(with zero hipster pretense). Now he vends everything from
hip hop and funk to classic rock and punk in south KC.
11539 Hickman Mills Dr., Kansas City
816-204-8840, facebook.com/GotWhatULikeRecords

The Hill
Photo courtesy of Cory Weaver

GREAT MAIN STREETS AND NEIGHBORHOODS

GET YOUR "FINS UP"
AT THE LAKE OF THE OZARKS

If you have lived in Missouri for any amount of time, the odds are pretty good that you have been to the Lake of the Ozarks . . . repeatedly. You probably have been there so many times that you wonder what new there is to do. The good news is that Jimmy Buffett took notice of the Ozarks and decided to put one of his famous resorts, Margaritaville, right there on the shores of the lake. Margaritaville now stands where the long-time favorite Tan-Tar-A stood as a legendary Lake resort for decades. Everything has been updated and given a new vibe, consistent with the songs we all know and love by Buffett. From the indoor water park to the outdoor dining and bars, you can find your cheeseburger in paradise nestled among 420 acres on the banks of the Magic Dragon Lake.

494 Tan-Tar-A Dr., Osage Beach
800-826-8272, margaritavilleresortlakeoftheozarks.com

OTHER MISSOURI GREAT LAKES

Table Rock Lake	Mark Twain Lake
Stockton Lake	Lake Wappapello
Smithville Lake	Pomme de Terre Lake
Warsaw Lake	

GET SQUARED AWAY
IN DOWNTOWN CLINTON

The historic square in downtown Clinton actually is Missouri's largest square, and it's packed full of activities, stores, and restaurants, making it perfect for a day trip. The square dates to the 1800s and retains its Victorian charm. In a matter of a few city blocks, you can check out the Visitors Center in the old Katy Trail Depot, the Henry County Courthouse, the Soldiers Memorial, and a historic bandstand and fountain, along with other relics that have been restored to the previous glory. The town puts on quite a show during Cruise Nights throughout the spring and summer months, hosts a Wine Stroll where you can check out numerous local eating and drinking establishments, and sponsors Christmas in Clinton, which gives you an amazing, small-town Christmas feeling.

clintonmo.com

GO TO
WHERE IT ALL BEGAN
IN MISSOURI'S FIRST TOWN

Sometimes you just need to see where it all started. When it comes to Missouri, that means Sainte Genevieve, along the Mississippi River. There are so many ways to do it right, whether you are a history buff, a food lover, a wine connoisseur, or just want a road trip for two. The Historic District is easily walkable, and is contained within the newly designated Ste. Genevieve National Historical Park. Just park near the old Main Street and you can see houses and businesses from the early 1700s like the Felix Valle House State Historic Site, the Linden House, and the Bolduc and LeMeilleur houses. There also are plenty of museums and cultural sites to see in close proximity. If food and drink are what you're after, you have to check out the historic Anvil Saloon and Restaurant, which is right in the middle of everything you will want to see and always promises an adventure!

Ste. Genevieve Welcome Center
66 S. Main St., Ste. Genevieve
800-373-7007, visitstegen.com

Felix Valle House State Historic Site
198 Merchant St., Ste. Genevieve
573-883-7102, mostateparks.com/park/
felix-valle-house-state-historic-site

Anvil Restaurant & Saloon
46 S. 3rd St., Ste. Genevieve
573-883-7323, anvilstegen.com

· ·

SEE WHY
THE DELMAR LOOP IS ONE OF AMERICA'S BEST STREETS

There are plenty of cool and hip places to hang out on a Saturday afternoon in Missouri. But only one street in the state routinely is named one of the coolest streets in America. Delmar Boulevard in University City, better known as The Loop, is iconic. It has the St. Louis Walk of Fame, it's the home of Blueberry Hill, and, according to the American Planning Association, it's also one of the Ten Great Streets in America. It is block after block of trendy restaurants, hip shops, and theaters that attract a little bit of everybody. So start early, plan to get a frosty mug of root beer at Fitz's and a burger at Blueberry Hill, do some bowling at Pin-Up Bowl, and see all the names of the St. Louisans that have become famous over the years and have been immortalized with stars on the pavement.

visittheloop.com

EXPERIENCE ITALIAN CULTURE
ON THE HILL

One of the most iconic neighborhoods in Missouri lies just south and west of downtown St. Louis and has become a tourist attraction, thanks in large part to a celebration of Italian culture. The area became well-known, thanks to the high number of Italian immigrants who settled in the area early in the city's history and formed a tight-knit community. This area of town now is bustling with authentic Italian restaurants and bakeries that attract hundreds of families every weekend. You can take a drive on Hall of Fame Place, or the 5400 block of Elizabeth Avenue, which is the street where Yogi Berra and Joe Garagiola grew up.

hillstl.org

TIP

Check out the recently completed fountain and park known as Piazza Imo. The Piazza sits directly in front of St. Ambrose Catholic Church and is a great place to relax, reflect, and enjoy the culture of the Hill. Grab a treat from Gelato di Riso just around the corner!

Missouri Baking Company
2027 Edwards St., St. Louis
314-773-6566

Vitale's Bakery
2130 Marconi Ave., St. Louis
314-664-6665

Marconi's Bakery
1913 Marconi Ave., St. Louis
314-773-8728, marconibakery.com

Volpi Foods
(home of prosciutto, salami and other cured meats,
with loyal customers across the country)
5256 Daggett Ave., St. Louis
314-772-8550, volpifoods.com

Gelato di Riso
5204 Wilson Ave., St. Louis
314-664-8488, gelatodiriso.com

DISCOVER
WHY DOWNTOWN CAPE GIRARDEAU IS A WINNER

A road trip to Cape Girardeau provides a good introduction to the state's Bootheel, a more Southern-feeling area than Missouri's urban centers. And this college town combines the "town and gown vibe" as well as any, with a great collection of shops and restaurants. Old Town Cape is a 2015 Great American Main Street award winner, and for good reason. The buildings in downtown date back to the Civil War, but have been revitalized with everything you need for a day of exploration, right there along the river in one of the coolest downtown areas in the state.

TIP

If you want to add a little Missouri history to your road trip, check out the Common Pleas Courthouse, high on the hill overlooking the Mississippi River and downtown Cape Girardeau.

Common Pleas Courthouse
44 N. Lorimier, Cape Girardeau
573-335-1631

REVISIT "THE DISTRICT"
OF DOWNTOWN COLUMBIA

The last time many Missourians walked around downtown Columbia probably was in college or during a visit to the campus. But downtown Columbia has experienced a renaissance as of late that makes it worth a trip all to itself! The vibrant nightlife, cool stores, and unique restaurants up and down East Broadway, coupled with the energy of the college crowd, give the downtown district the feel a Main Street is supposed to have. And if you happen to be there on a weekend when a big event is taking place, that's even better.

visitcolumbiamo.com

TIP

Make it a weekend and stay at the refurbished Tiger Hotel to get the full experience. The luxury, boutique hotel takes you back in time, and even has a speakeasy called the Vault to make the experience complete.

The District of Downtown Columbia
discoverthedistrict.com

The Tiger Hotel
23 S. 8th St., Columbia, MO 65201
573-875-8888, thetigerhotel.com

SUGGESTED
ITINERARIES

OUTDOOR ESCAPES

GREAT FOR KIDS

• •

SPORTY SPOTS

HITS FOR MUSIC LOVERS

• •

ACTIVITIES
BY SEASON

WINTER

Shop Posh at Country Club Plaza, 149

Chill Out with the St. Louis Blues, 69

Hoop It Up at the College Basketball Experience, 48

Feel the Vibe at the American Jazz Museum, 31

Get Inspired Divinely at the Cathedral Basilica, 116

SPRING

Take in Opening Day for St. Louis Cardinals, 64

Catch the Incredible Dog Challenge at Purina Farms, 36

Do Something Fishy at Bennett Springs, 63

Find the Luck of the Irish on Both Sides of the State, 101

Make a Pilgrimage to the Golf Mecca in the Ozark Mountains, 58

Laissez Les Bons Temps Rouler at Mardi Gras in Soulard, 77

SUMMER

Get Your "Fins Up" at the Lake of the Ozarks, 154

Do Dinner . . . and So Much More at Top of the Rock, 14

Celebrate Missouri at the State Fair, 132

Escape to the Fugitive Beach, 52

Scream for Missouri Ice Cream Parlours, 17

• •

ACTIVITIES
BY REGION

CENTRAL

EAST

• •

WEST

• •

NORTH

SOUTHEAST

• •

SOUTHWEST

• •

INDEX

• •